THE IMAGO DEI

CASCADE COMPANIONS

The Christian theological tradition provides an embarrassment of riches: from Scripture to modern scholarship, we are blessed with a vast and complex theological inheritance. And yet this feast of traditional riches is too frequently inaccessible to the general reader.

The Cascade Companions series addresses the challenge by publishing books that combine academic rigor with broad appeal and readability. They aim to introduce nonspecialist readers to that vital storehouse of authors, documents, themes, histories, arguments, and movements that comprise this heritage with brief yet compelling volumes.

THE IMAGO DEI
Humanity Made in the Image of God

Cascade Companions

Cascade Books
An Imprint of Wipf and Stock Publishers
199 W. 8th Ave., Suite 3
Eugene, OR 97401

www.wipfandstock.com

PAPERBACK ISBN: 978-1-4982-3340-8
HARDCOVER ISBN: 978-1-4982-3342-2
EBOOK ISBN: 978-1-4982-3341-5

Cataloguing-in-Publication data:

Names: Peppiatt, Lucy, author.

Title: The imago Dei : humanity made in the image of God / Lucy Peppiatt.

Description: Eugene, OR: Cascade Books, 2022. | Cascade Companions.| Includes bibliographical references and index.

Identifiers: ISBN 978-1-4982-3340-8 (paperback). | ISBN 978-1-4982-3342-2 (hardcover). | ISBN 978-1-4982-3341-5 (ebook).

Subjects: LSCH: Image of God—Biblical teaching. | Image of God—History of doctrines. | Theological anthropology. | Women—Religious aspects—Christianity. | Sex role—Religious aspects—Christianity | Disability—Religious aspects—Christianity.

Classification: BT701.3 P47 2022 (print). | BT701.3 (ebook).

THE IMAGO DEI

Humanity Made in the Image of God

LUCY PEPPIATT

CASCADE *Books* · Eugene, Oregon

For Murray Rae, mentor and friend

CONTENTS

ACKNOWLEDGMENTS

I BEGAN THINKING ABOUT this book many years ago after a conversation with Robin Parry, who encouraged me to undertake to write a Cascade Companion on this topic. So first I would like to thank Robin for suggesting this to me. It's taken me years to get to writing the book, and not only because I'm always too busy. I think it is partly because it is enormously challenging writing a *short* book on the imago Dei. Almost every idea I refer to represents volumes of writing, and there are many, many ideas I had to leave out. It feels hard to do the topic any justice at all, and yet, I'm persuaded there is value in summaries and signposts as a foundation for further exploration. I would like to thank the many students who have studied with me over these years of thinking, for their questions and their interest and delight in theology that helps me to think about how I communicate and makes me a better teacher. I also want to thank my staff team at Westminster Theological Centre. They pray for me as I write and rejoice with me when I finish! I'm hugely grateful for their support and patience with a sometimes distracted Principal. I'm especially grateful to Jasper Knecht, who read this through for me and left me helpful notes.

I can never thank Murray Rae enough. He is endlessly supportive, gracious, and generous with his time, and always makes my work better than it would have been without his input. He is someone who not only teaches, but also practices what I cite in the book as "redemptive theology," a theology that restores hope. He does this by treating those around him, but especially those who might otherwise be overlooked or ignored, as those who are made in the image of God and, therefore, worthy of dignity and respect. He is an inspirational professor of theology.

My deepest gratitude is always to my family, my four sons and now my four daughters-in-law and my husband, Nick. They are the context within which I think and write. They talk with me, laugh with me, and challenge me. Their love and support sustains me.

This book was written and finished during a pandemic and all the chaos that it brought. The world is still reeling from COVID-19, and we are now in the aftermath of the worst of it, but not even at the end, with what seems a multitude of deep-seated problems in so many nations. Now, more than ever, we need to work to reflect what it means to be made in God's image, indeed, to image God—to learn to receive God's love, to balance the scales of justice, and to treat others as precious in God's sight.

INTRODUCTION

THE DOCTRINE OF THE imago Dei, that human beings are created in the "image and likeness of God," is central to Christian life and practice and touches, perhaps even helps to form, every other doctrine of the Christian faith in one way or another. We do not think about God, in a Christian sense, as any other than the God who creates humanity in God's image. The content of this claim, however, is left largely undefined by Hebrew and Christian Scriptures and is not even mentioned in the creeds. However, the quest for what it *means* for human beings to be made in the image and likeness of God has never ceased to occupy theologians, clerics, and the laity, as people seek to understand this claim. The topic of what defines a person, or how we understand the essential core of what it means to be a human being (the *locus humanus*), fascinates us, and occupies a central place in many disciplines, not just theology. And theological reflection is affected by the conclusions of these other disciplines when we search for what it might be for the essence of a human being to be connected to or shaped by God. This quest and the conclusions that are drawn therefore are noticeably affected by the worlds in which we live: how we understand personhood in general, relations, human potential, psychology, philosophy, culture, politics, and so forth. Thus, throughout the ages the search for what it might mean for human beings to made "in God's image," has been understood in multifarious ways, and to some extent the doctrine evolves through time.

The shifting tides of how this doctrine has been developed over the years and how we ourselves answer this question tell us as much about what we think about God as they do about what we think about ourselves, of humanity and personhood in general, of those who share our faith, of those of other faiths, and of those of no faith at all. This is because this doctrine touches the heart of existence, communicating to us that at this heart is an indissoluble connection with God, the one who created us.

The locus classicus for this topic is Gen 1:26–27:

> Then God said, "Let us make humankind in our image, according to our likeness; and let them have dominion over the fish of the sea, and over the birds of the air, and over the cattle, and over all the wild animals of the earth, and over every creeping thing that creeps upon the earth."
> So God created humankind in his image,
> in the image of God he created them;
> male and female he created them. (NRSV)

We find other references in Gen 5:1–2, Gen 9:6, and Ps 8. In each of these references the Scriptures refer to humanity as a whole. There are also further references in the Apocrypha, where we find a more detailed explanation of what it means for humanity to be made in God's image in Sir 17:1–13, with additional references to humanity in God's image in Wis 2:23 and 2 Esd 8:44.

In the New Testament, "image" language is used almost exclusively in relation to Christ either with reference to Christ as the *eikon* (image) of God, or to humanity as refashioned into Christ's image and likeness (Rom 8:29; 1

Cor 15:49; 2 Cor 3:18; 4:4; Eph 4:24; Col 1:15; Heb 1:3). In Jas 3:9 we find a reference to those "made in the likeness of God," which refers to all humanity. In 1 Cor 11:7 there is an unusual reference to man alone as the "image and glory of God" whereas woman is designated as the "glory of man." In all this, however, the Scriptures do not tell us precisely the nature of this connection between God and humanity—wherein it lies and how it manifests in an individual person or in humanity as a whole—so this raises a multitude of questions. The following, in no particular order, are some of the questions that we consider in relation to what it means for humanity to be made in the image and likeness of God. In the course of the book, we will explore each of these in more detail.

1. In Gen 1:26, we find two Hebrew words used for humankind *tselem* (image) and *demuth* (likeness). In the Septuagint, they are translated into Greek as *eikon* (image) and *homoiosis* (likeness). From early on among Christian scholars there was a debate about whether these two terms were referring to distinct characteristics of humankind in relation to God, or whether they were, to all intents and purposes, synonymous.

2. Again, from early on, theologians have asked the question of whether humanity is made in the image of the Son or in the image of the Trinity.

3. In Gen 2, we have another creation story following Gen 1. Here the human being is formed out of the earth and then receives life as God breathes into the human's face or nostrils (Gen 2:7). This human being becomes man and woman when God takes a rib from the human being while he sleeps and fashions woman out of his being (Gen 2:21–22). Upon seeing the woman, the man cries out: "This at last is bone of my

bones and flesh of my flesh" (Gen 2:23 NRSV). One of the questions we will consider is, to what extent is the creation of humanity as "male and female" constitutive of the image? In other words, is there something essential in humanity as male and female that tells us what makes human beings like God?

4. Gen 3 tells us the story of the fall of humankind. The story of the fall raises a question about what happens to the image of God in humanity after the fall. Is the image completely destroyed, or does some vestige of the image remain?

5. In the Christian story, whatever has happened to the image in fallen humanity, it is fully restored in Christ. There are further questions, therefore, concerning the relation of the Genesis texts referring to all humanity and the New Testament texts referring to Jesus Christ. What is the relation of the imago Dei to the imago Christi? Does the imago Christi become the only expression of the image of God? Further to this, if we understand human beings as re-formed into the image of Christ, is this something that only relates to Christian believers? If not, how does the imago Christi relate to those of other faiths or those of no faith at all?

6. We are constrained, therefore, by the Genesis texts and others to having to make universal claims in relation to humanity as a whole, while at the same time, being constrained by the New Testament witness that defines the image of God with reference primarily to Christ. Thus, the doctrine of the imago Dei in a Christian sense may only be developed christologically. If we make the claim, however, that the imago Dei is given shape by Christ, we are then confronted with myriad christological questions concerning whose

Christ and which Christ ultimately shapes this doctrine. And once we have decided upon the answers to these questions, we are faced with the question of how *this* Christ (however we understand Christ), is imaged, if at all, in all humanity.

7. Another question is how we understand the imago Dei in relation to the nonanthropic world. The Bible singles out human beings as the ones who are made in God's image and likeness as distinct from other creatures, so wherein does this distinction lie, and how has this shaped the doctrine?

8. Connected to this previous question is the issue of how human beings as the image of God are related to the rest of creation and how we understand the command to have "dominion" over the creation given the destruction of our planet.

9. What part does the body play, if any, in our understanding of the imago Dei when the God in question is both triune and spirit and thus disembodied and without gender? Concerning this latter point of embodied existence are questions related to gender, sex, sexuality, desire, health, and disability.

As becomes obvious, questions abound! And this is really only a few of the questions we can ask of this doctrine. This volume is a short and largely descriptive volume. I do not subject each account to any detailed critique in any way, although I do bring out some of the problematic issues and lacunae associated with various accounts, as it is these that mean the doctrine is under constant revision. As scholars reflect on this doctrine from the perspectives of their own cultures, experiences, and knowledge of God and humanity, they bring new and valuable insights to the conversation.

As I have already mentioned, this companion is simply a brief introduction to some of the main perspectives on the imago Dei. For this reason, we will focus on questions pertaining to the imago Dei and not on theological anthropology in general. The two are obviously linked in that a Christian theological anthropology is usually founded on the doctrine of the imago Dei, but will also normally be a more expansive exploration of personhood in general, intersecting with philosophy, culture, politics, psychology, and so forth.

In addition to this, this companion has a specific focus on how the doctrine of the imago Dei has been broadly understood through the ages within the Western Protestant theological tradition and, therefore, has some significant gaps in relation to Majority World contributions to the discussion. There is much more that could and should be said from a global perspective. This book also has significant gaps in terms of the ground covered, partly because it is not possible to survey every contribution to the discussion, and partly because even in a comprehensive volume on this topic, the range of contributions to the history of interpretation spans so many disciplines, it would require multiple authors. As J. Richard Middleton writes, "to adequately discuss and situate this history of interpretation would require, minimally, expertise in Second Temple, talmudic, and medieval rabbinic Judaism as well as in the history of Christian theology and exegesis from patristic to modern times, including Christian speculation by nontheologians such as the humanists of the Italian Renaissance, among whom the imago Dei was prominent."[1]

Instead, this book is designed to be an introduction for students of the Western tradition, giving readers an overview of the major developments of thought through

1. Middleton, *The Liberating Image*, 39.

the ages with reference to some influential individual theologians or schools of thought when relevant. Readers will be able to use this volume to then explore aspects of this doctrine that pique their interest.

1

SUBSTANTIALIST AND
NOETIC PERSPECTIVES

INTRODUCTION

IN THE FIRST THREE chapters we consider, in turn, the three
main perspectives on the imago Dei that have dominated
the church's understanding over the centuries. In the subsequent two chapters, we will look at the ways in which
these views are deemed to be problematic and explore
some of the alternative perspectives offered in contemporary scholarship. Out of the main three perspectives, the
two predominant views are described as the substantialist
(or ontological) account and the functionalist accounts of
the imago Dei. John T. Swann classifies these as either (a) a
characteristic or condition of humankind or (b) a commissioning or commandment for humankind.[1] The third is a
relational account. In this chapter we consider the substantialist account.

1. Swann, *The Imago Dei*, 3.

9

For many centuries, the substantialist account of the imago Dei dominated the church's teaching, with theologians largely defining the image in terms of an attribute that human beings possessed that was believed to mirror an attribute of God. This is why it is called the substantialist or ontological account, as if we were able to identify an inherent and concrete aspect of human being that we share with God. Or in other words, the aspect or faculty of human being that is most like God. In this respect, whatever or wherever this was in a human being, it would have to be an aspect of human creatureliness identifiable in the whole of humanity. Neither the creation stories in Genesis nor references in other books of the Bible to the creation of humanity tell us precisely what it is that human beings *possess* that mean they bear God's image and likeness. However, it is clear from the text that whatever it is about humanity, it is something unique to human beings that they do not share with their fellow nonanthropic creatures. The animals, although created by God, are created neither in the same way nor for the same purpose. They do not receive the breath of God, nor do they converse with God in the way that humans do. They receive no instruction as to what they may or may not do in the garden, and no commissioning in relation to their role within creation. Thus, as part of attempting to locate the essence of the imago Dei in humanity, it was also thought that the aforementioned aspects of human beings were those that differentiated humans from animals. As Kathryn Tanner puts it, the substantialist accounts are ones in which humans are deemed to be "higher on the ontological scale of created beings by possessing certain faculties such as intelligence and will; their rationality, freedom from necessity, and capacity for self-determination." It is these faculties that make them like God.[2]

2. Tanner, *Christ the Key*, 1.

Other faculties that are sometimes identified as reflections of the image of God in humanity are the ability to love and be loved, spirituality, immortality, conscience, memory, language, and personhood. As many point out, however, the more we discover of the nonanthropic world, the harder it is to make a case for a sharp differentiation between human and animal faculties. As the early church wrestled with the question of what it was in humanity that was "like" God, there were two errors they wanted to avoid. The first was the mistake of anthropomorphizing God or bringing him down to our level. This is the age-old error of creating God in our own image. The second was the mistake of divinizing humanity and thus erasing the boundary between the infinite and ineffable God and mortal human beings. Both spring from the fundamental error of collapsing the distinction between the creature and the creator. From the beginning, those reflecting on the connection between God and humanity were adamant that orthodox Christian thought maintains this distinction between the two. Creation is not God; therefore, the creatures made in his image are both like and unlike him.

IMAGE AND LIKENESS

In the Introduction, we cited Gen 1:26–27 as the locus classicus for our thinking on humanity and the image of God. One topic under discussion is whether the two words used in Gen 1:26, image (*tselem*) and likeness (*demuth*) are synonymous, or whether they denote distinct characteristics of humanity, distinct modes of relating to God, or both. Scholars are divided on this issue. Some argue that because *tselem* indicates some physicality (sometimes referring to a concrete form such as a statue), it is referring to a copy or image of an original whereas *demuth* refers to the likeness or similarity to God in a less tangible form. This also communicates that human beings are not exact copies of God as it were. It is difficult to demonstrate conclusively that the writers of the text were making a strong distinction between the two concepts; thus many commentators identify Gen 1:26 as a hendiadys (naming a single reality using two expressions). What we can say is that together they tell the reader that humanity somehow resembles and represents God without being exactly like him.

Both Irenaeus and Thomas Aquinas make some distinction between the two categories of image and likeness, but more with reference to how humanity relates to God. For this they focus on the prepositions. Rather than translate the phrase as "in" or "according to" the image and likeness of God, Irenaeus uses the preposition "after" the image of God, and Aquinas chooses the preposition "to" the image of God.[3] These choices nuance the relation of humanity to God's image in slightly different ways from if we say that humanity is made *in* the image of God. In both cases (with Irenaeus and Aquinas), this is followed by the proposal that those who are made after or to the image, are then subsequently made "into" God's likeness in relationship with him through Christ. In my view, this reading of the text also gives a sense of movement *towards* becoming the image of God rather than imagining that humans possess the image solely as a static quality. We will come back to this idea in a later chapter.

THE RATIONAL SOUL

In early Christian thinking, it was the rational soul or psyche which was thought to be the faculty that mirrored

---

3. See Irenaeus, *Against the Heresies* 5.6.1, 5.16.1–2; and Aquinas, *Summa Theologica* 1.93.1 s.c.

something of God. It makes sense in an ancient context to identify this particular aspect of human creatures as the reflection of the image, as it was the rational soul where one would locate the powers of knowing and willing. This then is where one could find the capacity for rationality, freedom from necessity, and self-determination mentioned above. The fact that this was labeled as the *rational* soul is somewhat confusing for those influenced by modern Western thought. Many people in the West today associate the term *rational* with logical, dispassionate thinking, or something akin to that, and would perhaps view it as a solely intellectual term. In the early centuries of the church, however, the concept of the rational soul (the psyche) was more complex than this, and although it certainly was referring to the intellectual (in that the rational was also associated with the mind), it was mostly identified with the capacity that human beings were given by God in order to see him, know him, understand him, and love him. There is a different Greek word just for the mind, the *nous*, which corresponds to our understanding of the intellect alone. It was via the rational soul that humanity was able to apprehend God, so the psyche was where one could locate the point of connection with the divine. It is no wonder that this aspect of human being was deemed unique in the creaturely world.

Another modern perception of early Greek-influenced thinking is that it was overly philosophical and abstract in relation to the image and thus somehow divorced from the particulars of the biblical story. It is certainly true to say that the Greek influence on the development of the Christian faith lends one kind of philosophical perspective on God, but it would not be true to say that these philosophical deliberations were divorced in any way from the story of salvation. In fact, those who were writing in the first centuries of the church saw Greek categories of thought as aiding them in their thinking about how to describe the nature of God in a way that would faithfully tell the gospel story. The early theologians were, for the most part, also pastors. They were bishops, presbyters, and monks in the church and thus missionaries in their own world. The articulation and transmission of the gospel was their primary task, and battles against false thinking and teaching from within and without the church their primary focus. Early church thinking may appear to modern readers to be somewhat abstract, but once it is understood that theology was never abstracted from soteriology (i.e., how God brings salvation), it is easier to locate the debates in concrete concerns. It would also be a mistake to think that the church fathers all held to one homogeneous view of the imago Dei.

Irenaeus (c. 130–c. 202)

It is sometimes claimed that all early church thinkers saw the image as the rational soul and, therefore, in entirely nonmaterialistic terms, but this is not entirely true. Although the early church fathers prioritized the rational soul in relation to the image, this was not always seen to be at the expense of the material or bodily realm. Irenaeus emphasizes that human beings are a composite of spirit, soul, and body, all of which are significant in how we understand humanity as the image of God. As noted, Irenaeus makes a distinction between the two words *image* and *likeness*, with the term *image* relating to all humanity, and *likeness* reserved for those who are being made into the likeness of God in Christ. Thus, in his view, all humanity is made after the image of God, but it is only those who have received the Holy Spirit through faith in Christ who are being made into God's "likeness." More specifically, Irenaeus claims they are being modeled after the image and likeness of the Son into perfection. Those who are not in Christ have received the breath of life from God and so still have the image by virtue of having been created and formed by God. Only those who receive the Spirit of God through Christ receive God's likeness.[4] Hence, Irenaeus differentiates between two modes of the gift of the Spirit: the gift of the breath or Spirit of God that gives life to all human beings, and the gift of the Holy Spirit that gives eternal life to the Christ follower. The body, for Irenaeus, is essential to understanding the person as the image on the basis that the body is the temple of the Holy Spirit, the site of the presence of God. (Here he cites 1 Cor 3:16.[5]) The idea of the body as the location of the meeting place with God is further connected to the incarnation as when the Word became flesh he not only "showed forth the image truly, since He became Himself what was His image" but "He re-established the similitude after a sure manner, by assimilating man to the invisible Father through means of the visible Word."[6] Here the union of soul and body completes the image.

Athanasius (c. 296–373)

In his work, *On the Incarnation of the Word*, Athanasius states clearly that it is the possession of reason that makes human beings like God, and that this is reflected in the Word of God himself.[7] It is this connection of humanity to God himself through the Word that compels God to act to save humankind. The inherent worth of humanity to God means that for God to leave human beings to be carried off by corruption would be "unfitting and unworthy of

4. Irenaeus, *Against the Heresies* 5.6.1.

5. Irenaeus, *Against the Heresies* 5.6.2.

6. Irenaeus, *Against the Heresies* 5.16.2.

7. Athanasius, *On the Incarnation*, 6.

Himself."[8] For Athanasius, the capacity to know God with our reason is what differentiates human beings from animals. Furthermore, God gives us a share in his own image, in our Lord Jesus Christ, who shares both God's image and ours.[9]

As I noted, in most of the early accounts of the image of God there is an emphasis on the noetic (that which is related to the mind or intellect), but we see clearly in Athanasius's work how this is intertwined with the question of salvation. For Athanasius, human beings lost the knowledge of God, and therefore their relationship with him, through the fall. From that time, they turned to worship the created rather than the creator, coming under the influence of idols, which would ultimately lead to their destruction. To know and worship God is incorruptibility and eternal life, whereas to worship idols is corruption, nonbeing, and death. Thus, knowledge of God in Athanasius takes the form of re-ordered worship, which is restored in humanity through the revelation of God's mind exemplified in the Word of God made flesh, Jesus Christ. God comes in the perfect image of both God and humanity to re-create the image in humanity and to give the gift of eternal life. He does so because it is worthy of God himself to restore that which was made in his image; this is effected by God through coming in a body like ours. Only the Image of the Father is able to re-create the image of God in humankind, impart immortality, save humankind from death, teach them about the Father, and abolish the worship of idols.[10] The restoration of the image is through knowing God or perceiving and apprehending God again.[11] This is brought about through the forsaking

8. Athanasius, *On the Incarnation*, 6.

9. Athanasius, *On the Incarnation*, 11.

10. Athanasius, *On the Incarnation*, 19.

11. Athanasius, *On the Incarnation*, 11.

of idols and right worship, which restores a right mind in human beings, enabling them to apprehend God.

Gregory of Nyssa (c. 335–c. 395)

In *On the Making of Man*, Gregory of Nyssa has a similar emphasis on the noetic and the image, but also brings out the themes of kingship and rule in relation to the image. On the one hand, the image of God is reflected in the mind of humanity because God is Mind and Word. On the other, this unique role for humanity is lived out through the kingship and rule of human beings on earth. In his view, the royal role of man and woman explains why humanity is created last. God brings human beings into creation to enjoy all that he has prepared for them, that which he created specifically for their rule and reign. It is this status and calling that distinguish humanity from nonanthropic creatures—a distinction that Gregory makes much of. On the physical uniqueness of human beings, first he posits that human beings are the only creatures to walk upright in order that they may be closer to God. Secondly, he argues that the reason human beings have no physical advantage over other creatures is a sign, not of their vulnerability, but of their superiority. For Gregory, the need that human beings have of other creatures for protection and advancement signals the opportunity to exercise authority over animals and creation, utilizing what has been created in order to meet our needs. We will return to this idea in subsequent chapters and to how differently the role of humanity in creation is viewed by many today.

Another marked difference between ancient and modern times is Gregory's belief in a hierarchy of existence mirrored in the individual human being. In his view, the human being consists of three parts: vegetative, irrational, and rational. These correspond to the state of plants, animals, and humanity respectively, or what he describes as "carnal, natural, and spiritual" in ascending order. Although Gregory knows that human beings need to flourish on every level of existence, true spiritual flourishing occurs as the rational, intellectual, and spiritual aspects of the human being are drawn close to God. As this happens, the lower instincts (natural and carnal) are brought into order. Thus, in line with Athanasius, Gregory views human beings as born rational and capable of reason. A restoration of this rational aspect of the soul brings the carnal and natural aspects of existence under control and is, therefore, a restoration to the image of God. This has ethical ramifications, as it is the means by which virtue and righteousness are restored in the individual. Where the fall was a departure from virtue, beauty, and goodness, and thus the loss of the image, the return of humanity to God in Christ is a return to all these attributes. It is this, if you like, that restores a "right mind" and thus closely connects the restoration of the image to Christ-like behavior. In this way, we can see that the substantialist view of the image is closely connected to ethics.

There are two further points that Gregory makes in relation to the image that are worth noting. The first is his apophatic approach to the image, acknowledging that as human beings are made in the image of an incomprehensible and ineffable God, they too will have something about them that is incomprehensible and ineffable. Others have picked up this apophatic emphasis, arguing that although there is much we can say about the nature of human being in relation to God, there is also much that we cannot comprehend both in relation to God and in relation to humanity. Tanner, for example, writes that Jesus of Nazareth "displays in his life what it means to be an incomprehensible image in the flesh of an incomprehensible God."[12] This encapsulates both something of the mystery of God and of human being. "Becoming what we are only by way of the influence upon us of the divine image incarnate in human flesh, we become incomprehensible to ourselves in that what we have become is no longer explicable in simply human terms."[13] This, I think, is a salutary reminder when discussing the whole topic of humanity as the image of God—that it is not our task to find the comprehensive and definitive answer to the question of wherein this image lies. Furthermore, as Tanner points out, the doctrine by its very nature should always be able to accommodate something of the mystery of what is yet unknown. Any proposal for a "definition" of the imago Dei should take this into account.

The second point of interest is Gregory's perspective on sex and gender in the prelapsarian world (in the world before the fall). Gregory makes the point that human beings are made in the image of the Trinitarian God with Jesus Christ as the prototype of the perfect human image. For Gregory, although Jesus Christ is the prototype of humanity, we should still acknowledge that human beings are made in the image of the Triune God on the basis of the inseparability of the Father, Son, and Holy Spirit. Thus, he even refutes as heresy the idea that human beings are made in the likeness of only one person of the Trinity on the grounds that the Trinity is not composed of three distinct people.[14] These two foundational beliefs (1) in Christ as the prototype and (2) in humanity as made in the image of the Trinity lead Gregory to say that neither sex difference nor sexual union is essential to our image-bearing. With regard to sex difference, he makes the point that male and female

12. Tanner, *Christ the Key*, 55.
13. Tanner, *Christ the Key*, 56.
14. Gregory of Nyssa, *On the Making of Man*, 16.5.

are "alien to our conceptions of God," and thus are "peculiar attributes of human nature" rather than the definitive locus of godlike qualities.[15] Further, if we see Christ as the prototype of humanity, then we must follow Paul in his claim that in Christ there is neither male nor female. Here Gregory cites Gal 3:26–28.[16] And with regard to sex and procreation, Gregory's view is that this was introduced because of the fear of death, which had entered through the first couple's sin. In other words, procreation through sex was not essential to the first humans, but only a result of the fall.[17]

Augustine (354–430)

In *On the Trinity*, Augustine also argues that all human beings are made in the likeness of the Trinitarian God, even though, again like Gregory, he acknowledges that in relation to likeness, human beings are conformed to the likeness of the Son.[18] Augustine follows the strong emphasis on the noetic with the same focus on the mind that contemplates and knows God through prayer and worship; human beings are given a rational mind with which to contemplate God, in distinction from the animals. So here too we find a reference to the hierarchy of existence. Thus, it is not with the body and its features (associated as they are with the natural and the carnal) but with the mind that we image God.[19] The reason Augustine gives for this is that the image of God in humanity must needs lie in that which is immortal rather than in that which is wasting away.[20]

15. Gregory of Nyssa, *On the Making of Man*, 16.8, 16.9.

16. Gregory of Nyssa, *On the Making of Man*, 16.

17. Gregory of Nyssa, *On the Making of Man*, 17.

18. Augustine, *On the Trinity,* 12.2.6.

19. Augustine, *On Genesis*, 3.20,30.

20. Augustine, *On the Trinity*, 14.1.4.

Augustine is perhaps most famous for his psychological analogy of the Trinity where he maps the functions of
the human mind onto the Trinity in the form of memory,
understanding, and will as three modes of cognition that
function distinctly but inseparably. Augustine's Trinitarian
thought is not something we will discuss in detail here, but
it does give us a further indication of how the early church
fathers understood a natural connection between the mind
and the essence of God. We will return to the question of
whether humanity is made in the image of the Trinity or the
image of the Son in Chapter 4.

Another significant feature of ancient cosmology that
affects early thinking on the image is the idea of the movement of ascent and descent signifying the move toward and
away from God. This corresponds to the hierarchy of being
already mentioned in the three aspects of the human: the
carnal, the natural, and the spiritual (or intellectual). A hierarchical view of existence and the movement of ascent and
descent is a strong feature of Augustine's understanding of
the image, in which humans are called upward away from
the carnal and the natural and toward the spiritual or intellectual. This is linked to the idea of overcoming our base or
carnal instincts such as lust and greed, with the restoration
of the image carrying with it the strong ethical implications
that we have seen in Gregory of Nyssa. The intellectual is
not to be confused with a cold, rational perspective, but is
the site of wisdom and a superior knowledge of God, and
thus is the route to loving God and others. Hence, a restoration of the image will entail an ascent away from the
carnal (lustful, base instincts) and toward the intellectual
(synonymous with wisdom) to the unhindered contemplation of God.

Augustine became fascinated by 1 Cor 11:7 where we
read, "for man is the image and glory of God and woman is

the glory of man." He discusses this at length in *On the Trinity*. I will consider the significance of this verse in a later chapter but suffice it to say that Augustine ends up reading this allegorically—as man and woman together as a whole representing the higher and lower aspects of the whole human being before God. The key piece of Augustine's thinking here is that he understands Paul's statement through the hierarchy of being and symbol. Thus, men alone symbolically represent the higher, rational mind, even though they too possess the natural and carnal aspects of human being, and women symbolically represent the natural and carnal aspects of human being, even though they too possess the capacity for a higher existence. In Augustine's view, this justifies the covering of the woman's head in the presence of both men and God and the uncovering of the man's head in the presence of God and women. Augustine does not, however, read this verse as having any real bearing on the subordination of woman to man. Like man, woman is able to ascend to the full restoration as the image, and so Augustine sees male and female together as symbolizing the hierarchy of the human condition in its entirety.

Thomas Aquinas (1225–1274)

Thomas Aquinas largely follows Augustine and his predecessors in his thoughts of where the image of God in humanity lies; like them, he sees the image as that which distinguishes humans from animals.[21] In agreement with the church fathers before him, Aquinas understands the image via the noetic and gives an epistemological account of the image, in which the key to understanding how the image is present in humanity is linked to the knowledge of God. Here Aquinas distinguishes three tiers of knowledge.

21. Aquinas, *Summa Theologica* 1.93.5.

First there is the knowledge that is common to all, second an imperfect knowledge of God by grace, and third the perfect knowledge and love of God consisting in the likeness of God's glory.[22] He writes the following on the three categories of the image:

1. Inasmuch as man possesses a natural aptitude for understanding and loving God: and this aptitude consists in the very nature of the mind, which is common to all men.

2. Inasmuch as man actually or habitually knows and loves God, though imperfectly; and this image consists in the conformity to grace.

3. Inasmuch as man knows and loves God perfectly; and this image consists in the likeness of glory.

This Aquinas describes as creation, re-creation, and likeness. "The first is found in all men, the second only in the just, the third only in the blessed."[23] With the parallels we have already seen in others, Aquinas posits that it is with this intellectual nature that humanity is able to know, understand, and love God in the way that God in his mind and as Triune is able to know, understand, and love himself.

THE JOURNEY TOWARD GOD

As we can see, one of the recurring themes in relation to this account is the idea of progressive sanctification, as individuals draw closer and closer to God. In Chapter 3 we will explore how this took root and was developed within the Protestant tradition. In the Orthodox tradition, which has its roots in the first centuries of the church, this is expressed

22. Aquinas, *Summa Theologica* 1.93.4 Ans.
23. Aquinas, *Summa Theologica* 1.93.4 Ans.

through the concept of theosis, the idea of a human becoming godlike or divine the closer they draw to God. Dionysius the Areopagite in the late fifth to early sixth centuries defines *theosis* in the following way: "theosis is the attaining of likeness to God and union with Him so far as this is possible."[24] Generally, Western theologians are nervous that the doctrine of theosis blurs the creature/creator divide. This is addressed in Eastern thought through a distinction between God's essence and his energies, first formulated by Gregory Palamas (1296–1359). God's essence (his very being) is ineffable and incomprehensible, but his energies (his effects in the world) are seen and known. Thus, humanity is able to participate in the life of the divine through the energies but does not have access to God's essence. The question of how regenerate humanity participates in the life of God remains a much-disputed topic and not one that we will discuss in any detail here, but we will return to this topic in later chapters. The key point here is to note the assumption operating behind these accounts—that humanity is being made into the image and likeness of God in some progressive fashion. This is a dominant theme in many accounts of the imago Dei.

THE IMAGE AND ETHICS

In a later chapter, we will come to some of the difficulties associated with the substantialist view and specifically the idea of the image as the rational mind. To close this chapter, however, we will summarize very briefly some of the ways this view has been deployed ethically, contributing to a positive understanding of the place of human beings in the world. If the substantialist view is not sketched out in too

24. Dionysius, *On Ecclesiastical Hierarchy,* quoted in Russell, *The Doctrine of Deification*, 248.

much detail (i.e., if it rests on a simple claim that humanity, by virtue of being created human, is made in the image and likeness of God), it serves as the foundation for a number of ethical claims.

In its simplest form, the substantialist view speaks of the value of the existence of each human being due to the fact that they have the stamp of the creator. The idea that human beings bear *the* or *an* image of God can be extrapolated in a number of ways but is often used in a general sense to denote equality, unity, dignity and the sanctity of human life. Gen 9:6 is frequently cited as a text that supports the idea of the sanctity of life in relation to the image, prohibiting, as it does, the taking of a life. Those who protested the murder of George Floyd in 2020, the event that catalyzed the Black Lives Matter movement, bore placards declaring that George Floyd was made in "the image of God." It seems clear, in accordance with Gen 9:6, that the placards were declaring that no one should have taken his life by force. I presume it was this particular sense of the doctrine of the imago Dei that was expressed and understood through those placards. In other words, this short phrase did not need to be explained further but served as a synecdoche for a weighty ethical claim.

Alistair McFadyen identifies this definition and shared understanding as having "a long history of being deployed protectively to prevent or release human beings from dehumanising treatment."[25] In addition to this, although there is much criticism in the contemporary world of too sharp a distinction between humans and other creatures, there are still semantic indicators of how we understand acceptable and unacceptable behavior through the use of terms such as *humane*, *inhumane*, and *bestial* or *animalistic*. Humane behavior is compassionate or benevolent behavior. It denotes

25. McFadyen, "Redeeming the Image," 112.

a certain level of care, respect, and protection of the other. Inhumane or bestial behavior is behavior that displays a disregard for the value of human or even nonanthropic life, often including overtones of cruelty toward the other. In other words, just in popular culture, to be human rather than animal carries with it certain expectations as to how one should be treated and should treat other creatures. We will come back to some aspects of this discussion in the next chapter.

DISCUSSION QUESTIONS

1. If you were to have to identify an aspect of human being that you thought was most godlike, what would that be?

2. Does it make sense to you that early thinkers thought about the image of God as primarily located in the soul?

3. What more might you want to say about where God's image lies in humanity?

4. Do you think of human beings as superior to animals in any way?

2

KINGSHIP, PRIESTHOOD, AND STEWARDSHIP

INTRODUCTION

In this chapter we discuss what is sometimes called the functional, vocational, or missional view of the imago Dei. This perspective is rooted in a more detailed exegesis of Gen 1 and 2 than we see in the substantialist view, particularly focusing on Gen 1:1—2:4a. In the main, it is biblical scholars who espouse this view of the imago Dei, with slightly different emphases. For the most part, Old Testament scholars focus in particular on the Genesis passages and other references throughout the Old Testament, and New Testament scholars develop these themes christologically. Although, as we will see, there are some diverse accounts of the functional view, the overarching theme associated with this perspective is that humanity has a God-given role in creation that carries with it both an authority and a responsibility to mediate the rule, reign, and presence of God on the earth while under God's rule themselves. Scholars emphasize different aspects of this role. Some focus primarily on a royal role and others on a priestly role. Still others bring out the creative or artisan role of humanity in relation to God, and in recent years there has been a greater emphasis on human beings as stewards of creation in a more specifically ecological sense of stewarding well the resources within creation. Often these are intertwined into one account and cannot be easily disentangled one from another. The main point of these views is that they focus on the *purpose* of humanity's presence here on earth in the sense of what we have been called to do.

Clearly, there are ways in which this perspective might be developed in a universalist direction, in that one could make the claim that all human beings are called to a particular vocation in God's eyes whether they acknowledge they have been created by God or not. In other words, regardless of whether a person is in relationship with God, we could make a claim for their God-ordained purpose. However, for the most part, this view is propounded within a specifically Judeo-Christian framework in relation to God's covenant people, on the grounds that it is the ones who place themselves under God's rule and reign who are commissioned for the task. In this sense, the fall is seen as a falling away from the calling upon humanity as Adam and Eve reject the rule and reign of God to pursue their own desires and establish autonomy in rebellion against God's expressed command. This leads to disaster and brings forth a catalog of broken relationships—the relation of humanity to God, of human beings with one another, and of humanity with creation. Humanity's disobedience and rebellion establishes hardship, suffering, shame, endless toil, violence, the oppression of women by men, murder, and cycles of revenge. Thus, fallen human beings are unable to fulfil their calling and commission on the earth to image God. However, by coming under God's rule and reign (through adhering to

God's laws in the old covenant, and through coming under the lordship of Christ, baptism and the gift of the Spirit in the new covenant), the potential to image God is able to be restored.

A further feature of this perspective, therefore, is that it is frequently developed in a missional or ethical direction. Once it is established that the imago Dei in humanity lies in the calling to represent God among God's creatures, the theology of the imago Dei may be utilized to argue or demonstrate that the calling upon human beings is not simply to *be* God's image on the earth, but to enact an ethical and missional imperative, as God's image-*bearers*—to carry the presence of God to the world. The functional view, therefore, gives rise to a number of fruitful and generative theological anthropologies associated with kingdom theology, mission, and ecology, placing, as it does, a great weight on the capacity and potential of human beings as God's coworkers on this earth. In other words, there is a distinct emphasis in this view on human agency and cooperation with God. Whether in relation to royal, cultic, creative, agricultural, or socioeconomic spheres, the picture that is painted of humanity is that of a people who are commissioned to a representative and mediatorial role on the earth under the overall rule and reign of God.

Space precludes any detailed discussion of the various theological anthropologies arising out of each functional perspective. However, a pervasive theme in this discussion related to my point above is the idea that human beings are called to be the bringers of *shalom* or peace. If the effects of the fall are extreme disharmony, hostility, and the shattering of peace between human beings and God, human beings and one another, and humanity and creation, then the salvation of humanity, and the restoration of the image of God within, will result in the restoration of peace, reconciliation, and wholeness, or *shalom* on earth. Although this word *shalom* is normally translated as "peace," it has multiple connotations in Hebrew associated with the restoration of broken walls and with wholeness, completion, flawlessness, and healing. It is clear then how this view of the image of God provides a foundation for missional anthropologies especially in the light of the apostle Paul's emphasis on the gospel of Jesus Christ as the peace and reconciliation that is effected on the earth through the cross (see especially 2 Cor 5:11–21; Eph 2:11–22). Followers of Christ are then commissioned to bring about this peace or *shalom* as ministers of reconciliation in concrete ways in all aspects of life.

GENESIS IN CONTEXT

Many scholars argue that we cannot understand the claim that human beings are made in God's image and likeness unless we have a much clearer picture of what the writer or writers of Genesis intended to convey through the text in its own context. One of the ways to gain this clearer picture is to examine the first Genesis text in comparison to other writings of the ancient Near East in order to ascertain both how the Genesis creation stories conform to accepted patterns of its time and genre, and how it subverts them. In doing so, we are able to understand the unique picture given to us in Genesis of the creation of the universe by God as opposed to other creation myths and legends. There are now many scholars associated with this perspective as a general approach to the study of Genesis 1–2, so rather than discussing this topic through the lens of individual thinkers, we will refer to some overarching and recurring themes associated with this view with a reference to some specific writings on the subject.

Many scholars note that on the one hand there is a fundamental continuity between the creation stories in Genesis and Mesopotamian (Sumerian and Akkadian) material and Egyptian myths and legends; on the other hand, there are interesting contrasts. We will go on to note some of the overlapping intertextual themes in relation to creation and the building of a temple. However, one of the fundamental and significant differences between the Hebrew Scriptures and the contemporary literature is the role of humanity before God or the gods. It is generally acknowledged that in Cuneiform literature, human beings are created to serve the gods' needs and to do the work that the gods themselves do not wish to do. In stark contrast, however, as Middleton notes, "In connection with the priestly, cultic dimension of the imago Dei, it is further noteworthy that language of human service is entirely absent from Genesis 1."[1] Instead, we see a startlingly anthropocentric vision of creation, in which, as we have already noted, human beings are depicted as the crown of creation. Where all else that was created was "good," humanity is declared by God to be "very good." Not only this, but in contrast with its contemporary literature, Genesis presents us with an entirely democratic picture—all humanity is made in the image and likeness of God, not simply the king or ruler.

Thus John Walton notes that in contrast to other ancient accounts of humanity's role on earth, in Genesis the whole of humankind "serves the rest of creation as God's vice regent."[2] And yet many of the scholars who espouse this view make even greater claims. Walton is not alone when he goes on to add, "Among the many things that the image of God may signify and imply, one of them, and probably the main one, is that people are delegated a godlike role (function) in the world where he places them."[3] It is this godlike role that we will discuss in this chapter.

---

1. Middleton, *The Liberating Image*, 209.
2. Walton, *The Lost World*, 67.
3. Walton, *The Lost World*, 67.

Certainly, theologies of the image that focus on the rule and reign (or even the godlikeness) of humanity raise concerns with regard to imperialism, hubris, vanity, and all the negative connotations that accompany such a paradigm. I will not discuss that in detail in this chapter but will go on to discuss critiques of the dominant views of the imago Dei more thoroughly in Chapter 4. As we have already noted, it is a misreading of early church theologies to claim that they ignored the functional view entirely. Theologians of the first few centuries did not reject the idea of humanity as kings and priests in the world; it is simply that their notion of the imago Dei as a concept tended to be explicated with reference to human attributes rather than human functions. We saw, however, that Gregory of Nyssa has a strong emphasis on the royal nature of men and women conferred upon them by God as his image and so will begin there.

THE CREATION OF GOD'S ROYAL TEMPLE

Those who explore Gen 1 and 2 in its context bring out the theme of God as the one who creates a royal temple or sanctuary in which to dwell. A number of indicators in the Genesis text liken the creation of the universe to the construction of a temple. First, the text tells us that God breathes and speaks the creation into being. The idea that God thinks, speaks, and breathes the universe into being indicates that this God is a ruler, bringing a cosmic temple into existence, from which he will rule and reign. Further evidence for this can be seen in the preponderance of references and allusions to the number seven evident in many different aspects of the text. Not only are there parallel accounts in ancient Near Eastern literature of the creation of temples that foreground the number seven, but the number seven also occurs in biblical accounts about the construction of Solomon's temple.

The number seven can be found in the detail of Gen 1—2:3 in the repetition of the phrases "it was so" and "God saw that it was good." Middleton notes the following: there are multiples of seven evident in the crafting of the text— thirty-five occurrences of the word *God*, twenty-one of *earth*, and word counts in multiples of seven for the entire text (469 words). The seventh day has a total of thirty-five words while, as Middleton notes, the precreation preamble in 1:1–2 has "21 words: 7 words in 1:1 and 14 in 1:2."[4] As Middleton avers, this sevenfold structure "seems to have cultic, liturgical significance and may well be associated in some way with the Jerusalem temple."[5] He also sees resonances of temple references to creation in Isa 66:1–2 where we see that God has built a cosmic temple for his dwelling.[6]

Clearly, the most obvious occurrence of seven is the seven days of creation if we include the seventh day of rest. Moreover, it is significant that the seventh day is one of rest, as it was well known that gods took up "rest" in their temples once the temples were completed. Walton makes the point that this seventh day of rest for God would, therefore, have clearly communicated a temple theme to an ancient Near Eastern audience. They would have been accustomed to the notion that divine beings, once they have created their temples, come to take up their rest in their own dwelling places. Walton makes the point that this is not rest as in putting one's feet up and doing nothing; this rest entails a king or ruler taking up residency in their palace, from which they will now begin their rule and reign.[7] These are

4. Middleton, *The Liberating Image*, 83.

5. Middleton, *The Liberating Image*, 83.

6. Middleton, *The Liberating Image*, 81–82.

7. Walton, *The Lost World*, 71–73.

all indicators then that the Genesis text is telling us of a royal sanctuary out of which God and his icons function. In addition to this, seven is a significant number in the Jewish world, as it signifies wholeness and completeness, which interweaves with the theme of *shalom* mentioned above.

A further reference to royal imagery may lie in the plural "Let us make . . ." There are a number of explanations given for this plural. Some claim this is an early reference to the Trinitarian God or to plurality in God himself, while others see an allusion to some type of polytheistic perspective. A likely allusion, however, is to a heavenly court or angelic divine council, which we also find referenced in multiple places in the Old Testament (Genesis, Job, Psalms, Chronicles, Exodus, Samuel, Kings, Isaiah, Jeremiah, Ezekiel, and Daniel). This royal imagery in relation to the divine angelic council is brought out clearly in Ps 8:5–6, "You have made them a little lower than the angels and crowned them with glory and honor. You made them rulers over the works of your hands; you put everything under their feet." In contrast to certain versions of the substantialist view that we explored in the previous chapter, underlying some versions of the functional view held by biblical scholars is a consensus that *tselem* (image) refers to a visible, corporeal representation of God himself in human beings. As a result, there is more potential with the functional or missional view for a theology of embodiment, and to see the body as a significant aspect in how we define the imago Dei. Rather than diminishing the somatic dimension of life, we are able then to place a greater emphasis on physical presence and physicality in general. We will return to this theme in Chapter 5, on contemporary views of the imago Dei.

In sum, those who see the image of God in royal terms claim that humanity has a unique role in creation to rule in a kingly office over nonanthropic creatures and the planet, if not the universe. Middleton, one of the main proponents of a royal functional reading of the imago Dei, writes, "Humans are *like God* in exercising royal power on earth" and he adds, "The divine ruler *delegated* to humans a share in his rule of the earth. Both are important ways of expressing the meaning of the imago Dei."[8] According to this view, then, the purpose of humanity is rule, but firmly under God's sovereignty and in submission to him.

It is worth stating the obvious here—that the church has not always exercised and does not always exercise power in a "godlike" way, and the abuse of power in the church, attributable perhaps in part to a distorted theology of the imago Dei, has caused untold suffering. As we mentioned above, in the Old Testament the people of God are called to follow God's law as his image-bearers on earth, and in the New Testament these laws are fulfilled in the person of Jesus Christ. Thus in the new covenant, to be an image-bearer is understood christologically, which gives us a particular perspective on power. Jesus Christ is not only the second Adam who himself models perfect obedience and submission to God the Father, but he also confers authority upon those who are submitted to himself to carry out the will of God on earth. This authority, however, is antithetical to the kind of power and authority exercised by earthly rulers, and is to be characterized by humbling oneself under God, engaging in self-sacrifice, and preferring others. In imitation of the Savior Christ, whom Christians follow, serving as God's representatives on earth is meant to be submissive, self-denying, meek, and nonviolent. Jesus teaches his disciples explicitly on this in the Gospel of Luke where he references ruling and kingship in the context of serving and waiting on others:

8. Middleton, *The Liberating Image*, 88 (italics original).

24 A dispute also arose among them as to which of them was considered to be greatest. 25 Jesus said to them, "The kings of the Gentiles lord it over them; and those who exercise authority over them call themselves Benefactors. 26 But you are not to be like that. Instead, the greatest among you should be like the youngest, and the one who rules like the one who serves. 27 For who is greater, the one who is at the table or the one who serves? Is it not the one who is at the table? But I am among you as one who serves. 28 You are those who have stood by me in my trials. 29 And I confer on you a kingdom, just as my Father conferred one on me, 30 so that you may eat and drink at my table in my kingdom and sit on thrones, judging the twelve tribes of Israel." (Luke 22:24–29)

HUMAN BEINGS AS PRIESTS

A second functional view of the Imago Dei, which has similarities with the royal view (in that it is also founded on the representative and mediatorial roles of humanity), is an understanding of human beings as God's priests on earth. This is sometimes developed in tandem with the royal view, which I will come to, but the idea of human beings as primarily in a priestly office places a very different emphasis on the role of humanity than if we were simply to focus on the royal role. As we have seen, the temple imagery of Gen 1 invites us to see the creation as God's sanctuary. It follows, therefore, that God's representatives would be given priestly duties to perform within the temple. This is often explicated with reference to Gen 2:15 where God places Adam in the garden to work it and take care of it. Adam is then given a companion who is bone of his bone and flesh of his flesh in Eve, and they are cocurators. Thus, John T. Swann makes a case for the preeminence of the priestly role in relation to the image: "Since the image of God is best interpreted as a representation of cultic interest, the human dominion over Creation should be viewed as a form or ministry or curation."[9]

An emphasis on humanity as priests gives rise to a number of rich themes in relation to the image. The first is that image-of-God theology is then organized primarily around worship. The purpose of humanity's presence on earth is not only to worship the creator but also to lead creation in praise and worship. The Scriptures make it clear that creation is able to praise God and, indeed, does so (Ps 19:1–4; 148; Isa 55:12; Rev 5:13). Jesus even claims that if human beings fail in the praise and worship of God that is their duty, creation will spontaneously praise God anyway (Luke 19:40). The theme of priesthood foregrounds the establishing of the Sabbath, the day of rest and worship, as the culmination of the work of creation. Swann brings out a plethora of narratives associated with this cultic role.

Firstly, the imagery of priesthood accords to humanity the role of bringing about purity and cleansing from sin and contamination. Secondly, the priest is one who is enabled to transmit the blessing of God down the generations. And thirdly, there is the duty of caring for the creation as the temple of God. Swann summarizes the basic qualities of priesthood as ordination, curation, mediation, edification, and sanctification.[10] These traits are rooted in the holy priesthood itself. In Swann's view, Exod 19 and the commissioning of the people of God through Moses to be a "priestly kingdom and a holy nation" (v. 6) is the key text. Hence, priestly imagery encompasses a corporate aspect whereby the *whole* people of God are summoned to holiness. Swann

9. Swann, *The Imago Dei*, 25.

10. Swann, *The Imago Dei*, 183.

cites both the Old Testament and New Testament references to this in Lev 11:44–45 and 1 Pet 1:14–16 with the repetition of the phrase, "you shall be holy, for I am holy." Thus we see the theme of the imago Dei and the priesthood trace a continuity from creation, through the Old Testament, and to the formation of the church in the New Testament, as the people of God are formed as a kingdom of priests, mediating God's presence on earth. We will return to the theme of sanctification and holiness in Chapter 3 with respect to the christological, relational views of the image.

A ROYAL PRIESTHOOD

Although some scholars argue for the primacy of either the royal or the priestly role in relation to the imago Dei, there are those who argue that the two should not be played off against each other but held together for a fuller understanding of the biblical portrayal. Swann argues for the primacy of the priestly view, and Middleton focuses mainly on the royal view but also understands the image as both these concepts working together. "In the cosmic sanctuary of God's world, humans have pride of place and supreme responsibility, not just as royal stewards and cultural shapers of the environment, but (taking seriously the temple imagery) as priests of creation, actively mediating divine blessing to the nonhuman world."[11] Carmen Imes also brings these two themes together in her covenantal, functional view of the image, which she relates to the concept of "bearing God's name."[12] In her view, humanity is elected to "bear God's name," which means to live out God's laws on the earth as his "treasured possession" (or *segullah* in Hebrew).[13] Imes

---

11. Middleton, *The Liberating Image*, 90.

12. Imes, *Bearing God's Name.*

13. Imes, *Bearing God's Name*, 31.

draws a distinction between those who bear God's image, which relates to all humanity, and those who bear God's name, which relates to those in covenant with God.[14] Those in covenant with God, who are not just in his image, but bear his name, are called to be a kingdom of priests and a holy nation, "serving as his ambassadors to the nations."[15]

Quite clearly, however, and as Middleton and Imes would be quick to acknowledge, there are multiple ways that the church throughout history has failed to mediate a healing and restoring royal rule or to be a divine blessing to the world. At times, the church has instead been responsible for appalling destruction. This is not to say that some Christians throughout the ages have not also been channels of healing and peace to the world, but not in any pure, unadulterated, or consistent sense. If the people of God are truly called to this role of royal and priestly image- and name-bearing, then we have a long way to go in understanding how to live this out. Contemporary scholars are often only too aware of this and so are careful to present a chastened account of the functional view.

STEWARDS OF CREATION

Many contemporary scholars have reacted against the idea of rule and dominion in relation to humanity's relation to creation because of the visible and dire consequences of human beings' exploitation of the created world. Not only has this led to catastrophic climate change and the extinction of species, but human greed has led to a lack of resources for large swaths of the earth's population. That many in the world go hungry while animals are farmed intensively to supply Western greed for cheap meat at the same time that

14. Imes, *Bearing God's Name*, 164–65.
15. Imes, *Bearing God's Name*, 31.

people in the West waste obscene amounts of food is rightly identified as sinful and corrupt. The link is often made between this behavior and a fundamentally hubristic and entitled view of human being. Whether distorted perspectives on the imago Dei fuel this kind of behavior is difficult to establish incontrovertibly, but we can say that there are resources in the Judeo-Christian tradition to challenge it.

Sandra L. Richter rejects the concept of dominion, arguing instead that humans were created in order to be stewards of God's good creation, called to respect and protect creation (the garden) under God. In her view, it is this that constitutes what it means to live lives as a reflection of God's image. With reference to Gen 1 and 2, she notes that *adam* "(a collective term meaning 'humanity') was given the privilege to rule and the responsibility to care for this garden under the sovereignty of their divine lord."[16] She builds on the notion of stewardship with reference to the Old Testament—specifically to the laws given to Israel in Leviticus and Deuteronomy relating to economic growth, oversight of wild and domestic animals, farming practices, and care of the poor. The calling of humanity is to succeed in "constructing the human civilization by directing and harnessing the abundant resources of the garden under the wise direction of their Creator."[17] Richter makes a strong argument that humanity, as the steward of creation, could so curate and care for the world that there would be abundant resources for all because this is how God has designed the world. Richter describes this is in ideal terms: "progress would not necessitate pollution, expansion would not demand extinction. The privilege of the strong, would not necessitate the deprivation of the weak. And humanity would

---

16. Richter, "A Biblical Theology," 69.

17. Richter, "A Biblical Theology," 69.

succeed in these goals because of the guiding wisdom of God."[18]

Richard Bauckham issues a similar critique against the notion of rule and dominion, bringing out the need for humanity to understand itself as wholly dependent upon the created world. He makes the important and obvious point that although human beings are powerful forces in the world, there is a sense in which creation is still stronger than humanity and is able to exert its own power over us with sometimes catastrophic effects. As much as we have tried, humanity has never been able to "master" creation and all that it throws at us in terms of disease, predators, and natural disasters. Bauckham writes, "Realising our membership of the community of creation dispels the illusion of omnipotence and enables us to think more realistically about the power we do have."[19] He also makes the valid point that as well as curating creation in terms of engaging with and caring for the world, we should also think in terms of "letting be," restraint, and enhancement. We share the earth with other creatures who also have a right to be here.[20] It was fascinating to see the environmental changes of the global lockdowns of 2020 and 2021 when people stopped flying and travelling by car. There was a dramatic decrease in sewage and industrial effluents in rivers, the oxygen levels in river water increased dramatically, noise level was significantly reduced worldwide, there were lower greenhouse emissions and improvement in air quality. We saw fish inhabiting the canals of Venice, animals roaming through cities, and the noticeable increase in birdsong. This

18. Richter, "A Biblical Theology," 69. For an expanded account of Richter's biblical theology of creation care see also Richter, *Stewards of Eden*.

19. Bauckham, *Bible and Ecology*, 90.

20. Bauckham, *Bible and Ecology*, 36.

all supports Bauckham's plea that some of what humans should *do* to support the environment is nothing at all.

AN ETHICAL RULE?

Modern scholarship in relation to the functional view of the imago Dei emphasizes the subjection of humanity under God and the idea that the earth belongs to God and not to us (Ps 24:1). The land and our lives are a gift, not an entitlement, and anything that human beings do on this earth is to be lived out in conformity to the image of Christ and the Christian ethic to love our neighbors as ourselves. In recent years, we have seen an increase in human care for the treatment of animals and a trend towards not harming (or what is tantamount to torturing) animals for our own use. This has not necessarily been driven by Christians, but many Christians have now joined the cause. This takes different forms in the call for the merciful and nonexploitative treatment of the animal kingdom. There are many now who are fully vegetarian, refusing the idea that humans should rear and slaughter animals for food. Others reject the use of animals for any human need whatsoever and are vegans, while others take a less stringent approach advocating for an end to intensive farming and the overconsumption of meat. With all this in mind, and given the sinful propensity of human beings, debate will no doubt continue as to whether royal and priestly language is helpful, and if so, in what ways.

GOD AND CREATURES AS ARTISANS

A final functional view arising out of Genesis is the idea of God and humanity as artisans or creators. This is partly a version of the substantialist argument in that it is predicated on the idea that God not only creates but is the creator.

Human beings, therefore, who are made in his image, not only create but are inherently creative and are creators. Early church thinkers noted these parallels but would have been careful to point out that God alone can create out of nothing. Human beings, in contrast, are able to create only out of the stuff they are given that is created by God in the first place. This raises questions about the term *cocreator*, which is often used in this context. This could mean that human beings are creative as the God who made them is creative, or it might imply that God needs humanity to complete his creation, which would be a disputed idea. Nevertheless, the idea of the imago Dei expressed in human creativity is yet another rich and interesting theme. God is the supreme creator, an artisan who both carefully and skillfully imagined his creation in the first place, and then willingly brought it into being with love and care. Thus, to be made in his image is to be an essentially creative creature, and God equips humanity to continue the task of creatively forming all aspects of life. J. Richard Middleton describes it thus, "God has . . . started the process of forming and filling, which humans as God's earthly delegates, are to continue."[21]

The idea of human beings as cocreators can be developed in a number of different directions. It can be understood in terms of aesthetics—that human beings create things of beauty in art of all kinds: fine art, building, music, poetry and prose, gardening, cooking, and so forth. In this connection, the examples of Bezalel and Oholiab are often cited, two artists chosen and anointed by God to "engage in all kinds of crafts" in the building of the Israelite tabernacle (Exod 31:1–11). God's image in humanity could also be understood in terms of humanity's ability to invent. There is no doubt that human beings are endlessly inquisitive and resourceful, seemingly constantly engaged

21. Middleton, *The Liberating Image*, 89.

in inventive pursuits in order to progress in medicine, engineering, technology, architecture, and production of all kinds. As Gregory of Nyssa noted so many centuries ago, human beings are essentially and physically quite weak and vulnerable in the world compared to other creatures but are clearly intellectually equipped to utilize all the resources around them to protect themselves and to improve their quality of life.

As we saw the negative sides of the paradigm of ruling and reigning, so we also see negative aspects of human beings as creators. Human beings can create things of beauty and healing but are also skilled at creating the means of destruction. We are able to use our creative and inventive abilities to form weapons that will maim, kill, and destroy. Arguably, these are not creative abilities at all but de-creative abilities, but the principle stands. This raises a similar question: How we can claim such potential good on behalf of human beings when they are able to carry out such evil? We see here again that the functional view of the imago Dei is wholly dependent upon placing human potential under God's sovereign rule and reign, following a Christlike and cruciform pattern.

CONCLUSION

In Chapter 4 we will revisit some of the difficulties associated with the functional view in more detail. In conclusion, however, I wish to highlight some of the positive aspects of the functional view in all its forms. The first is that functional views of the imago Dei place a high value on the potential of a human life, and interpreted in the right way they serve as a strong foundation for ethical living. If the people of God are genuinely those who are called not only to serve in God's kingdom but to play a part in ushering in the kingdom of God through the enactment of God's love, mercy, compassion, and justice, then this issues a great challenge to the church. This highlights the potential of a life lived in submission to God. Whereas some will understandably be nervous about the impact of the royal or the priestly view of the imago Dei on the proud, the powerful, and the entitled of the world, the downtrodden, the disadvantaged, and the marginalized often need to hear about these aspects of the divine image in humanity. We noted in the beginning of this chapter the clearly democratic message of Gen 1 and 2. All humanity is made "in the image of God"; thus all people, all sexes, all races, and all ages are made to be appointed as royal priests in God's temple, palace, and kingdom. These are theologies that not only bring out the worth and dignity of human being on the earth; they also provide incentives for taking up caring and creative roles on earth.

DISCUSSION QUESTIONS

1. How do you feel about the idea that human beings are given "dominion" over creation as God's vice regents?

2. Out of the three roles that we have seen in this chapter (kings, priests, and artisans), which picture communicates most to you and why?

3. If you belong to a Christian community or church, are you satisfied that you as a community understand the nature of what it means to represent God on earth?

4. If you are not satisfied as a community with your collective understanding of what it means to bear God's image on earth, what changes would you like to make either to your understanding or to the ways you represent God as a community in the world?

3

RELATIONAL MODELS OF THE IMAGO DEI

INTRODUCTION

As I NOTED IN the previous chapter, it would be misleading to imagine that the relational aspects of the imago Dei were not in circulation before, say, the Reformation, when it is often claimed they came to the fore. All the noetic and epistemological models we discussed in the first chapter are predicated upon the relationship of humanity to God in one way or another. This relationship grows as a person grows in the knowledge and love of God in accordance with the apprehension of the nature of God via the rational mind. The knowledge and love of God reaches its fulfilment in and through the beatific vision and the participation of humanity in the divine Triune nature for eternity. Moreover, the kingship, priesthood, and stewardship models are equally predicated on the relation of God to humanity and vice versa. Thus we use this term *relational* here in a slightly different context, referring to the imago Dei in specifically relational concepts—relational concepts that are features of the imago Dei rather than simply consequences of salvation. Here, relationship is what defines the image.

There are many permutations of the relational model of the imago Dei: the fundamental paradigm is that the image of God in humanity resides in the fittingness and capacity of a human being to be in a relationship with God, or in the nature of the relationship itself, or in both. In other words, these views can be worked out either with reference to the potential within humanity or with reference to an actualized relationship both here and in the eschaton, or with reference to both the potential for relationship and an actual relationship. A relational understanding of the imago Dei can also be extended to include a thoroughgoing relational ontology. A relational ontology entails the claim that human beings are only who they are as *beings in relation* to one another as well as to God. The restoration of the image, therefore, is the restoration of a relationship with God that forms the foundation for a fully human existence that takes shape through reconciled and loving relationships. However, a full-blown relational ontology is not a claim made by all relational models. Thus, with relational models, the image of God is realized or fulfilled through participating in a reconciled relationship with God and possibly also with one another. In this chapter, therefore, I discuss the image in relation to covenant, Christ, the Trinity, kinship, and friendship.

We noted in the Introduction that concepts of the imago Dei have evolved over time and are never totally divorced from cultural, political, and historical concerns. Hence, ideas about how humanity is made in the image of God and in what way that manifests in human beings are often connected to the context in which those ideas were born. In the first few centuries of the church, it is probably true to say that theological reflection was dominated by concepts around the Word and the Mind of God, with little attention paid to any alternative idea of something like the heart as the center of a person. In addition to this, the bodily or carnal aspects of human being were relegated to a lower order and often depicted as the site of conflict in relation to sanctification and holiness and seen to be stumbling blocks to drawing near to God. This is not to say that issues around embodiment were neglected altogether, or that the affective aspects of life were ignored, but just that the noetic and epistemological concepts were privileged over others. It was also in these early centuries when traditions of asceticism and celibacy were held in high esteem, and when the goal of the Christian life was understood in terms of escaping the carnal elements of existence for a higher, contemplative plane. Attaining to the image of God, therefore, came to be defined by the idea of an ascent or upward climb away from the conditions of this world toward the divine. As these, often dualistic, ideas took root in Western theology, they were further worked out in later centuries in individualistic terms. Hence, we see Western theological accounts, to their detriment, marked by dualism and individualism in the modern era while we also see these foundations challenged in postmodern times.

The relational model in some of its versions can serve as a welcome corrective both to models of the imago Dei that privilege the mind over the body and to individualism. However, we cannot make this claim for all relational models, as some models continue to focus mainly on an individual believer's relationship with God with a focus very much on the spiritual aspects of a person rather than an earthly existence. We see shades of this in the moral-relational models of the Reformation, which we will turn to first; but before we do, we will discuss the context in which these ideas were born.

BACKGROUND TO REFORMATION THOUGHT

Before we discuss the turn to the moral-relational model of the Reformation, a brief overview of the historical context is in order, as there were some significant developments with respect to the status of the human being in the world following the Middle Ages—developments that represent some key shifts in thinking. Placing these ideas in context helps us to understand the background to how and why we think about the image of God in the West as we do today.

The Renaissance, which spans the centuries between the Middle Ages and the Early Modern period (roughly 1350–1600 CE, but that can also be placed later) marks a new perspective on the nature and role of humanity in the world and, on the whole, reflects a new optimism regarding the inherent potential of a human being. Humanist thought emerged and blossomed during the Renaissance when intellectuals looked back to classical Greek and Roman sources for an understanding of human being. This gave rise to a great emphasis on the innate nature of human freedom, reason, dignity, and power. Humanist thinkers resurrected the ancient Greek idea of "man as a microcosm," or literally a "little world" in a person, reflecting the macrocosm of the universe. Where the universe was understood as a physical world animated by the Logos, human beings were bodies animated by the soul. On top of this, world events lent themselves to Europeans discovering a sense of their own capabilities to control and conquer.

We see then a number of underlying concepts persisting in the Western tradition. First, we see the dualism of soul and body, which has dominated many accounts of the imago Dei in one way or another through the centuries. We will return to this. Secondly, in these Renaissance centuries and beyond, there is a hubristic move that elevated White European, males as both normative and superior versions of the imago Dei. Much of this is informed by the world-events of these centuries, as they were centuries of discovery on every level. In 1453, the fall or conquest of Constantinople to the Ottomans marked the end of the Byzantine Empire, which saw the dispersal of Greek-speaking intellectuals throughout Europe. This, in turn, fueled the growing interest in Bible translation from Greek into vernacular languages, which would later feed the appetite among Reformers to put a Bible in every hand. This was significant in widening the opportunities for many more people to become scholars of the Scriptures. The following centuries saw the discoveries of Copernicus (1573–1543) and Galileo (1564–1642), which marked the move from geocentrism to heliocentrism, signaling the advent of, literally, new worldviews. And scholars in all disciplines were growing in their confidence of what could be known of the natural world.

These were also centuries of exploration and expansion. Naval fleets grew as did naval routes in and out of Europe. With the discoveries of new worlds came European colonization, trade routes, and empire-building. Along with all of this came the beginnings of distorted theologies of the White man's supremacy and entitlement, and this had a direct impact on theologies of the imago Dei. These were centuries of the slaughter and enslavement of Black and Brown people by people of European heritage, growing racism, and the denigration of other non-White ethnic groups and women and in relation to the doctrine of the imago Dei. There were those who were deemed lesser images because of their skin color or sex, providing a warrant for their subjugation, enslavement, abuse, and murder. It is important not to gloss over these aspects of the theological thinking of these centuries as some of these aspects persist to the modern day. We will return to these themes in Chapter 4.

MORAL-RELATIONAL PERSPECTIVES ON THE IMAGO DEI

As the Renaissance was flowering in Europe, the Reformation was also born. And whereas the Reformation could probably not have emerged without the Renaissance, there were significant differences between the optimism of humanism and the pessimism of Reformation theological anthropologies regarding humanity's natural state. The Reformation was a reaction to systemic corruption within the Roman Catholic Church, specifically targeting the sale of indulgences—whereby priests would accept money for the remission of sins and release from purgatory. In 1517, Martin Luther disseminated his Ninety-Five Theses, making the point that repentance is a matter of the heart and lived out in lives that are obedient to God's word. The assurance of salvation comes, not from the absolution of a priest who has accepted money from the sinner, but directly from God through the cross of Christ. The Reformers called the church back to what is referred to as the "five solae" of the Reformation: sola scriptura (Scripture alone), sola gratia (grace alone), sola fide (faith alone), solus Christus (Christ alone), soli Deo gloria (glory to God alone). With these we see the beginnings of a shift away from a faith mediated through the priesthood and the Roman Catholic Church. The Magisterial Reformers continued to value the role of the priest and the church, but nevertheless, there was a move towards the idea of the full reliance on God himself in Christ and by the Spirit to provide all that human beings need to live a life of faith and obedient discipleship to God. Thus, although there is a wide range of views among Protestant denominations on the significance of the priesthood in general, on ordination and the nature of the church, nevertheless the five *solae*, by and large, continue to characterize Protestant theology.

There were many upheavals in thought in relation to doctrine during the Reformation, although the image of God was still seen primarily through a substantialist lens. Calvin, for example, speaks of the soul as the "proper seat of the image."[1] There were, however, new emphases during this period in relation to the image, which are discussed below. As this is simply a brief overview, we cannot deal with all the nuances of the many great thinkers of this time, so will draw out a few common themes.

One of the issues that divides theologians is the question of whether the image of God in fallen humanity is completely lost or destroyed, or whether there remains a vestige of the image in some form. Even then, if the image is deemed still to be present, there are different opinions as to whether that image is present but completely distorted, or whether there is some natural light or goodness remaining. In general, the emphasis during this period among Reformers was, on the one hand, the total corruption (total depravity) of fallen humanity whereby the image was either lost altogether or thoroughly deformed; and, on the other hand, the full and complete restoration of the image in and through Christ. Reformation accounts of the imago Dei were therefore thoroughgoing christological accounts of the image. In addition to this, where we have seen an emphasis on virtue in the early substantialist accounts, this comes into greater relief with the Reformers arguing, as

1. Calvin, *Institutes* 1.15.3.

they did, that the restoration of the image in Christ and the imputation of righteousness to the sinner will give rise to a corresponding and growing obedience to Christ in the life of a disciple. Hence, these are moral-relational perspectives on the imago Dei.

The Reformers' perspective on the human condition was very much influenced by Augustine. On the one hand, therefore, the fallen reason and will were understood to be utterly corrupted and thus incapable of naturally apprehending God or choosing the good. On the other hand, however, faith in Christ and union with him were understood to restore the faculties of individuals in order to orient them toward God. A new emphasis during this period was the primacy of a believer's relationship to Christ shaped by the five solae mentioned above. Thus, what unites the thinkers of the Protestant Reformation is both a fundamentally pessimistic perspective on the fallen state of humanity and the full assurance of salvation that a believer gains through faith and trust in Jesus Christ. Whereas the image of God in humanity is once either totally obscured or completely lost, it is imparted once again through the first image-bearer, Christ. Jesus Christ is seen to be both the archetype and the prototype of the image, and through union with Christ, he imparts his own image to the penitent sinner who trusts in the cross of Christ for salvation. Moreover, through the cross of Christ and the gift of the Spirit, God is able to sanctify the worst of sinners by grace alone. There is nothing that a person should or even could do to effect the transformation to the Christlike image apart from repenting, believing, and trusting, while even the ability to do this is a gift from God. Similarly, obedience to God can only be lived out through the presence of Christ in a believer and never through the natural efforts of the person themselves.

The general pessimism about the fallen state of humanity that marks Protestant Reformed thought is not mirrored in the same way in Roman Catholic thinking, which represents a more optimistic understanding of the natural, albeit fallen, state of humanity. The debate centers on whether human beings have a *capax Dei*, a natural capacity for God or not, associated with the image of God within. In other words, if humanity is made in the image and likeness of God, does this mean that there is a natural capacity to know and love God that persists within sinful humanity, despite the fallen state? Is there something within fallen humanity that is still able to respond to God because human beings are created for a relationship with him? In Reformed Protestant thought, as Karl Barth famously declared in a response to Emil Brunner, the clear answer to this question has been, "No!"[2] The rejection of the idea of a natural capacity for God stems from the fear that this would lead to a weakening of the all-sufficiency of Christ for salvation. If we have the capacity to apprehend God apart from the revelation of God through Christ and his atoning sacrifice, as Barth saw it, the heart of the gospel is lost.

It is important to understand, therefore, that the power for transformation into the image of God was seen to lie in the cross and resurrection of Christ, the grace of God toward humanity, faith in Christ, and the gift of the Spirit. God himself, through himself in Christ, imparts holiness and brings forth obedience as he confers his glorious image on those who are being saved through Christ. Although ideas such as total depravity or the complete destruction of the image may sound harsh to modern ears, it should be noted that the restoration and renovation of the person, in relation to Christ, was understood to be full and complete. John Owen makes the point that the depravation of nature

2. In Brunner and Barth, *Natural Theology*.

affects minds, wills, and affections, and is thus total. In his view, however, this should give us greater confidence that it will be our entire nature that will be renewed, including our souls and bodies. In Christ, we are given a new understanding, a new heart, and new affections. Owen himself cites Eph 4:23, 24 and Col 3:10 as foundational verses for this view of the image.[3] A person, in Christ, is able to put off the old self with its thoroughly corrupt desires and practices and put on the entirely new self in Christ. The Reformers took the promises of Scripture seriously in their view that someone could truly become a "new creation." It is important to understand total depravity in this light.

One of the key ideas here is that what a person does not own in the first place cannot then be taken away from them. The full restoration of the image rests in the relation to Christ and in one sense is perpetually borrowed from him, but is a full restoration nonetheless. The image is restored through justification in Christ, which includes adoption, assurance of salvation, resurrection and eternal life, and sanctification by the Holy Spirit, which includes the mortification of sin, the renovation of our natures, obedience and duty to God—and succor through trials and temptations. Even though there was an understanding that this renovation could not be complete in this life, there was an expectation that the restoration of the image would be evidenced in lives lived out in the knowledge and love of God, obedience to Christ, purity, righteousness, and holiness. Hence, the moral-relational model.

3. Owen, *The Works of John Owen*, 3:418–19.

FURTHER CHRISTOLOGICAL
RELATIONAL MODELS

There are a number of christological relational models of the image, one of the most prominent expositions of which is Karl Barth's. Barth's view of the imago Dei is thoroughly rooted in the person of Christ as well as the concepts of both covenant and election. In addition to this, Barth has an added relational aspect to his perspective in his insistence that male and female together constitute the image. Thus, he has both vertical and horizontal relational aspects to his view of the imago Dei. Barth also develops his theology of the image into a complex theological anthropology. In relation to this, Marc Cortez summarizes Barth's perspective in the following: "Jesus alone determines what it means to be human because (1) His humanity grounds ours eternally through God's eternal decision to be God-for-us-in-Jesus (election); (2) His humanity grounds ours redemptively through the covenantal faithfulness that both maintains our humanity and reveals true humanity; and (3) His humanity grounds ours existentially through the divine summons that we all receive to likewise enact covenantal faithfulness in the world."[4] In addition to this, Barth sees the male/female relation as integral to living out life as the image of God.

Barth's theology of the image is worked out through the framework of Martin Buber's "I–Thou" paradigm, with human beings restored as the image of God as they respond to the divine command that summons them into covenant partnership and fellowship. Barth sees humanity as God's counterpart, the repetition of the divine life—its copy and reflection. For Barth, coming into the coexistence and co-operation of covenant relationship with God is the fullness

4. Cortez, "The Madness in Our Method," 20.

of existence and humanity's freedom.[5] Barth writes, "As God offers man humanity and therefore freedom in fellowship, God summons him to prove and express himself as the image of God—for as such He has created him. This is the deepest and final basis on the form of the divine command which we now have to consider."[6]

For Barth, the I–Thou relationship of the Father and Son is the principal relationship within which humanity relates to God. Thus, Christ's response is a response "for us," and it is in him and him alone that humanity is called into fellowship with God. Furthermore, it is only in the complementary relation of man and woman that the image is complete. There is some confusion in Barth's work as to whether this is fulfilled simply through men and women coexisting together, or whether this is fulfilled specifically through marriage. In the end, he focuses primarily on the marriage relation, which, for Barth, reflects the covenantal I–Thou of the Father/Son relation. Here he goes into great detail, enumerating a theology of what he claims is the equal but asymmetrical relation of husband and wife, the active and the passive, the head and the body—which, in his view, is the complete, relational, covenantal image. We will come back to some of the problems associated with this idea in Chapter 4.

There are many other versions of christological relational models of the image articulated by systematic theologians and biblical scholars alike. In these, Christ is the principal image-bearer, and human beings are restored to the image as they are conformed to the image of Christ. As we noted before, Christ is both the archetype and the prototype of the image, but this, of course, raises the question of

5. Barth, *Church Dogmatics*, III/1, 185.

6. Barth, *Church Dogmatics*, III/4, 117 Also see Barth, *Church Dogmatics*, III/1, 191–206.

how we understand the person of Jesus Christ in relation to the Gen 1 narrative. Clearly, the Jesus Christ of history, the fully divine and fully human person, is not in evidence in any overt sense in the Genesis text. On the question of why the prototype is not chronologically prior, Oliver Crisp appeals to the eternal nature and purposes of God. The human nature of Christ is "eternally in view, as it were, in the mind of God logically prior to his ordination of all subsequent human beings."[7] Thus, he claims, this "provides the basis for a Christological gloss on Gen 1 that makes sense of the New Testament claims about the relation between Christ as the principal image-bearer, and fallen human beings as those that are being conformed to the divine image by being united to Christ."[8] In Crisp's view, therefore, we might see the image, not as something that Christ comes solely in order to renovate or repair, but as something that Christ himself "instantiates as the archetype and divine *eikon*. On this way of thinking, human beings are made in the image of God *by being made in the image of Christ*."[9] We could classify this view as an eternal christological view of the image. Crisp summarizes: "God eternally ordains that Christ be the archetype of human beings. The creation of human beings is in the 'image' of Christ, as embodied rational animals capable in principle of being hypostatically united to a divine person."[10]

In a form related to both Barth's and Crisp's christological frameworks above, Manfred Hedley develops a christological perspective on the imago Dei that he calls "covenantal eikonism," rooted in the book of Colossians. Colossians is a key text for christological relational

---

7. Crisp, "A Christological Model of the Imago Dei," 227.

8. Crisp, "A Christological Model of the Imago Dei," 222.

9. Crisp, "A Christological Model of the Imago Dei," 223.

10. Crisp, "A Christological Model of the Imago Dei," 226.

perspectives on the image, as Hedley enumerates. Not only does the apostle Paul state in this letter that Christ is the *eikon* of the invisible God, the firstborn over all creation, but Paul says that Christ now dwells in the faithful, as the hope of glory (Col 1:15, 27). The status of being seated with Christ in the heavenly realms has already been established for those who place their trust in Jesus Christ (Col 3:1). This then is the reason Paul gives for the imperative to love, forgive, and bear with one another, "for you have died, and your life is hidden with Christ in God" (Col 3:3). The renewal of all things has begun in Christ and has concrete ramifications for humanity, and from there, for all creation. Here, Hedley draws out Paul's view of what is given to humanity in Christ, by which human beings are established in who they are as images or *eikons* in relation to Christ as partakers of the covenant. This he sees in terms of new life characterized by redemption, reconciliation, and re-creation. As human beings participate in Christ's death and resurrection, they are drawn to faith, hope, and love, as well as sharing in the blessings of Christ's identity. They are given the fullness of God's presence, the life-giving power of resurrection, authority, and unity.[11] According to Hedley, these are understood as concrete gifts to humanity, resulting in a wholly new way of living.

John Swinton develops a christological view of the image in a different vein, based on what he calls "soteriological objectivism."[12] This is driven by reflection on those who have suffered severe neurological damage, so much so that they do not recognize themselves and are recognizable as the person they were. To this extent, they lose part of their former selves. For Swinton, this raises questions about who we *truly* are, and how that might or might not relate to the

11. Hedley, *The Colossian Image*, 198.

12. Swinton, *Becoming Friends of Time*, 187.

image of God and our personhood. He understands Paul's phrase of being "hidden with Christ" from a different perspective. In his view, salvation has been accomplished for us in Christ and is irreversible; it is secured for us as it were beyond ourselves. "This way of thinking also helps to secure our identity by locating it as lying outside the boundaries of our fragile bodies."[13] Thus, Swinton posits that who we truly are is properly hidden in Christ and still to be made manifest in glory.[14] This is resonant of some of the apophaticism that we referred to in Chapter 1. The heart of the image is, therefore, a mystery waiting to be revealed.

HOLINESS AND THE IMAGE

This raises interesting questions in relation to whether there are or even whether there should be visible signs of the imago Dei within a human being in this life. Is it a status that has been won for us that should be visible in some way? Is it simply present in all human beings, or is it something yet to be revealed? Is it a hidden aspect of our natures, or a new identity that will transform us and those around us for all to see? Both Bruce McCormack and Craig Blomberg argue for the image as holiness, which links back to the view of the image and virtue that we saw in the first chapter. This raises further questions around whether we are speaking of the imago Dei as the imitation of God (*imitatio Dei*) or the imago Dei as the imitation of Christ (*imitatio Christi*) and what we mean by differentiating between those two phrases.

Any moral-relational view of the image will also assert that there will be visible changes within a person as the image is restored in them. McCormack opposes the

13. Swinton, *Becoming Friends of Time*, 188.
14. Swinton, *Becoming Friends of Time*, 191.

substantialist view, embracing both a functional and relational view as he states that the imago Dei "is holiness." McCormack cites Lev 19:2 and the call to God's people to be holy as he himself is holy. This is a theme that then emerges in Jesus's Sermon on the Mount, a theme summed up in Matt 5:48. In McCormack's view, being conformed to the image of God has concrete, ethical implications, as God's people are called to live out holiness in obedience arising out of "kenotic, self-giving love." [15]

Craig Blomberg adopts a similar stance from a New Testament perspective. Rather than espousing a view of total depravity, he posits that human beings retain a vestige of the image of God even though they have been corrupted and have the potential for "committing acts of unspeakable evil." [16] He argues, therefore, that human beings are created with the capacity for moral behavior even though this can only be fully realized in Christ. [17] So for Blomberg, being made in God's image and likeness is what makes human beings uniquely qualified to exercise the role of being a force for holiness and goodness in the world. [18] Returning to Colossians, he asserts that Col 3:5–17 "demonstrates that Paul is talking about holy, moral and upright living" in relation to the image. We are to put off sin and put on Christ. Thus, the result of "sharing Christ's glory turns out to be living moral and upright lives." [19] This will be reflected in loving relationships, justice, and sacrificial living.

15. McCormack, "Panel Discussion at Los Angeles Theology Conference, 2015."

16. Blomberg, "True Righteousness and Holiness," 68.

17. Blomberg, "True Righteousness and Holiness," 68.

18. Blomberg, "True Righteousness and Holiness," 73.

19. Blomberg, "True Righteousness and Holiness," 79–80.

THE IMAGE AND THE TRINITY

Thus far in this chapter we have surveyed only christologi-cal perspectives on the image. The early church fathers held differing views as to whether the image of God in humanity is a reflection of the Son or the Trinity, and this debate persists. Irenaeus places the emphasis on a christological image whereas Gregory of Nyssa strongly refutes this idea on the grounds that the persons of the Trinity are not three distinct people. If humanity is made in the likeness of the Son, it must be made in the likeness of the whole Godhead in that the Son is the image of the invisible God.[20] Augustine also has a Trinitarian understanding of the image drawn from his perspective that the Trinity is analogous to a human mind, encompassing memory, understanding, and will. He sees Trinitarian patterns (*vestigia trinitatis*) in humanity and creation, which reflect God's being.[21] Centuries later, Thomas Aquinas follows Augustine in a Trinitarian perspective on the image.[22]

There are different Trinitarian perspectives, however, that have come to the fore in recent years, rooted in the idea of the Trinity as a social concept in relation to the image. This comes in different forms. Most are agreed that God is both one and three, with the three persons of the Godhead relating to one another in mutual love and glorification. This social view, however, claims that the oneness of God consists primarily of the three persons in relation rather than in their shared essence. This view of the Trinity is then mapped on to human relations, which are deemed to reflect something of the essence of existence both in God himself and in human being. Colin Gunton is a proponent of a

20. See Gregory of Nyssa, *On the Making of Man*, 16.5.

21. Augustine, *On the Trinity*, 12.2.6.

22 Aquinas, *Summa Theologica*, 1.93.5.

fundamentally social view of God and humanity, arguing for a fully relational ontology both in God and in humanity. God as Father, Son, and Holy Spirit is who he is as a being in communion and thus demonstrates to us the relationality at the heart of existence. As Gunton argues, human beings are what they are only in relation to one another.[23] To be made into the likeness of God's image in this view, will entail a healing of relations and engagement with those who are both not us and also are unlike us. Gunton develops this point with regard to reconciliation with those who are seen to be other.[24]

John Zizioulas, from within the Orthodox tradition, similarly argues for a perspective on the image of God as relational or social.[25] Zizioulas appeals to patristic sources, particularly the Cappadocian Fathers, for his emphasis on the threeness of God. For Zizioulas, as for Gunton, the relational is foundational to existence, as both God and humanity are "beings in communion." However, Zizioulas's theology is rooted in a very different ecclesiology from Gunton's. Whereas Gunton sees a relational ontology that has more of a community (even communal) and less hierarchical structure, Zizioulas respects his own ecclesial commitments to the episcopal hierarchies within the Orthodox Church. He holds to a high view of the bishop's role in shaping the body of Christ and in mediating Christ to the people. This raises interesting questions as to how relational structures within God are imposed upon human relations, and here we see a number of difficulties.

What has become clear in recent years is that the social model of the Trinity applied to human relations can

23. See Gunton, *The One, the Three and the Many*; and Gunton, *The Promise of Trinitarian Theology*.

24. See especially Gunton, *The One, the Three and the Many*.

25. See Zizioulas, *Being as Communion*.

be developed both hierarchically and nonhierarchically, depending on one's prior decision as to whether there is a hierarchy or not within the Trinity. For example, on the one hand, those such as Jürgen Moltmann or Miroslav Volf see both the nature of the Triune community and the nature of the ecclesial community as entirely mutual and nonhierarchical.[26] On the other hand, however, there are those who hold to the eternal subordination of the Son to the Father, who then map this, not just onto the church, but onto all male/female relations—with the male representing the authoritative Father and the female representing the submissive Son.[27] These are radically opposed views. We will discuss this further in Chapter 4. For this reason, and others to do with the worry that we might lose sight of the oneness of God, there are a number of critiques of this view of the Trinity and the resulting models of human relationality.[28]

Whether we perceive the image primarily in christological or Trinitarian terms will probably depend upon how we understand the essence of a human life and where we place the emphasis of what it means to live a life in relation to God. If we see the image as located in the mind or psyche, it is easier to envision the image as reflecting different aspects of the incorporeal Trinitarian God, as we can imagine three immaterial aspects of our own beings in one person such as Augustine's memory, understanding, will. Similarly, if we see the essence of human being as a light or spirit or breath given to all humanity, then the concept that this might be

26. Moltmann, *The Church in the Power of the Spirit*; Volf, *After Our Likeness*.

27. See for example Grudem, *Systematic Theology*, chapters 22 and 47.

28. See for example Holmes, *The Holy Trinity*; Kilby, "Perichoresis and Projection."

where the image of the ineffable God can be found becomes imaginable. God is spirit and his spirit resides within. However, if we place our emphasis on the embodied existence of a human in the material world, we might lean more toward a christological framework, as it is in the person and life of Christ that we see a human existence that mirrors our own. From this perspective, we might even associate the concrete actions of Jesus with the image and hold him up as an exemplar of image-bearing. This is behind the thinking of the image as *imitatio Christi*. Thus, viewing the image through a christological lens seems more compatible with human lives lived in the here and now and embodied existence, and perhaps lends itself to a more concrete exposition of what that image might look like. To some extent, the social model of the Trinity applied to the doctrine of the image of God takes a similar approach but with an emphasis on the nature of God rather than on the person of Christ.

Whatever we decide regarding the social model of the Trinity, one of the challenges for theologies of the imago Dei is working out both the individual and corporate aspects of this doctrine. It is not satisfactory to have a theology of the imago Dei that is solely applicable to individuals or to individuals alone in their relation to God without an understanding of what this means for human beings in community. It is understandable that many have turned to a Trinitarian perspective to draw out this aspect of the image. On this question, it should be noted, however, that a christological model is not by necessity individualistic, nor does it preclude the idea of the image as community. There are, to be sure, individualistic symbols in relation to the image, as we have seen in Chapter 2 (such as the symbols of prophet, priest, and king). However, Jesus taught that to be made in his own image is to love God and love our neighbor. There is no understanding of being made in the image of Christ that does not entail relationship. If we think in terms of the restoration of the imago Dei in Christ, this should also bring to mind an understanding of the image in corporate terms such as the body, the temple, the *ekklesia*, and a holy nation—all of which explain participating in the image of Christ as a collective, built up in relation to one another into Christ. In line with this thinking, the concept of the image in relation to kind and kin, or family, is a powerful one, and one that many see as foundational.

KIND AND KIN

Catherine McDowell argues that the image of God should be understood in terms of correspondence, kind and kin, as referenced in Gen 5:1–3.[29] Here we see that just as humanity is made in God's image, so Seth is created in the image of Adam.[30] The image, therefore, is primarily a familial term. As she notes, when human beings are created in Gen 1, God is humanity's nearest kin, and this kinship is analogous to the father/son relation. Thus, she avers, "To be created in the image of God is to be God's kin, specifically 'son,' with all the responsibilities and privileges sonship entails."[31] Needless to say, the language of "sonship" is problematic for women unless one sees this in symbolic rather than literal terms, and purely in relation to status. As a metaphor in relation to loving relationship, commitment, heirship, and inheritance, it is still possible, in my view, for this metaphor to speak to all people, although this will clearly need some explanation. If being made in the image of God means that all humanity, male and female, occupy the position of the beloved firstborn son in relation to the Father, with all the

29. McDowell, "In the Image of God."
30. McDowell, "In the Image of God," 35.
31. McDowell, "In the Image of God," 30.

privilege and status of the heir, it strikes me as important that the depth of this metaphor is retained and applied equally to women.

McDowell makes a further point that the language of sonship in the Old Testament overlaps with the language of kingship, as the idea of the divine sonship of the king can be found in the Old Testament and in extrabiblical references. This too is a powerful image, and, again, if applied to women, carries with it all the connotations of rulership so often associated only with men. On this note, we find the early church fathers less rigid regarding the application of masculine and feminine imagery—first with respect to God, whom they often describe in feminine terms, but also with respect to women, whom they might describe in traditionally masculine terms in order to denote their strength and resilience as disciples.

The language of sonship clearly has many Old Testament and New Testament resonances and is a rich seam throughout the Jewish and Christian Scriptures. Furthermore, it has theological significance primarily in relation to Christ and for understanding our relationship with God, our relationships within the family of God, and our relationships with those not in that family. The language of sonship is picked up by the apostle Paul and becomes a strong theme with regard to the adopted sons of God being conformed to the image of the natural Son, Jesus Christ. All the inheritance of the natural son is passed on to the adopted sons: a relationship of intimacy with the Father, the gift of the Spirit, the eternal riches of the kingdom of God (Rom 8:17; Gal 4:7; Eph 1:18, 2:6–7; Tit 3:7; 1 Pet 1:3–5). Furthermore, this picture has implications for how we relate to one another within the church. The language of the family of God, brothers and sisters, with Jesus as our brother and God as our Father, is such a dominant metaphor in the church and serves to shape and frame how we understand our obligations and responsibilities. The fact that we cannot disassociate one from another in the family of God is essential to our understanding of who we are and of what our commitments are to one another (See 1 John 3:11–17). This refers back to my previous point about christological perspectives on the image as inextricable from community and communion. Thus, any moves toward reconciliation and unity, so needed in the church, will be informed by this picture.

McDowell makes a further point though, arguing that all human beings "are members of God's clan and are therefore kin to one another."[32] In her view, this applies to the whole of humanity, and so she claims that the obligation of care and responsibility is extended to our fellow men and women via the shared image and shared identity. This has a missional and ethical element to it as she writes, "Israel was to live as God's royal sons and representatives before the watching eyes of the nations so that others would find a relationship with God irresistible."[33] In my view, the kinship perspective has stronger connotations than friendship, although they are not mutually exclusive. Finally, we turn to friendship.

FRIENDSHIP

The idea of the image dwelling in the capacity of human beings to be friends with God has its roots in both covenant concepts and kind and kin. It is evident in both the Old Testament and the New Testament and should be taken into account in relation to image theology. It is not, however, such a dominant theme as others we have noted and

32. McDowell, "In the Image of God," 37.
33. McDowell, "In the Image of God," 43.

so perhaps cannot carry the weight of all aspects of the image. In Gen 12:1 Abram is called to leave his own kin and his father's house and to go to a land that God would show him. This is the beginning of Abram and his kin's relationship with God, out of which comes the original covenant, formed with Abram as the father of many nations. Abram is called a friend of God (2 Chr 20:7; Isa 41:8; Jas 2:23). Moses too is called a friend of God (Exod 33:11; Deut 34:10). Jesus extends this friendship to his disciples, which we see most clearly in the Gospel of John's Farewell Discourses (John 13:34–35, 15:15). The theme of friendship is different from the familial theme, as it carries with it the sense of commitment as a choice rather than as a duty. It seems to me that this view has clear pastoral implications, especially in a Western world where loneliness is a chronic problem. This theme has also been taken up in relation to disability studies, most notably by Swinton.[34] The move towards friendship and the emotional connection that this portrays is helpful in order to avoid an overly noetic or individualistic account, and to highlight a relational ontology. In addition to this, the theme of friendship resonates with normal aspects of real life and brings to the fore the affective side of existence. Friendship is constituted by mutual love and voluntary commitment. Good friendships strengthen over time, weather the ups and downs of life, and nourish our emotional lives. Unlike blood relations, we remain friends with people because we choose to love them and choose to forgive them and to receive forgiveness from them, and so imagining that this is how God might view us as made in his image has great value.

---

34. Swinton, *Becoming Friends of Time*.

CONCLUSION

As we have seen, there are many benefits to understanding the imago Dei through the language of relationship. These views also raise questions. One of the questions is whether this relationship, whatever it is founded upon, needs to be reciprocal? Does the relationship that we have with God as a result of being made in his image require a response from us in order to be instantiated? Are these relationships static or dynamic? Are they a given, or do they need to be nurtured? Moreover, are there behavioral characteristics that go with each of these pictures? Is this a way of *being* before God, or is it a way of *living*, or both? We will turn now to some of the difficulties that are raised with the substantial, functional, and relational perspectives on the image.

DISCUSSION QUESTIONS

1. Have you had any experience of the idea that the White European male represents the image of God in a more perfect way than other representations of humanity?

2. Do you have a preference for viewing the imago Dei through the lens of the Trinity, through the lens of Christ, or through some other lens? Why do you hold your preference?

3. Can the language of "sonship" make sense to women?

4. In your opinion, what other aspects of relationship that were not discussed in this chapter might shed light on how humanity as imago Dei relates to God?

4

DISPUTED ISSUES

INTRODUCTION

It has become clear by now just how diverse the perspectives on the imago Dei really are, with many different emphases and nuances in relation to how we might understand what it means for human beings to be made in the image of God. The biblical texts—both in terms of the specific references to the image in Genesis and throughout the canon—give rise to multiple perspectives. In many ways it feels as though we have been left only clues from which we deduce what we are able, leaving the topic open to much debate. In addition to this, as questions in relation to what it means to be a human being and how we define personhood evolve and change in society, so does our understanding of what it means to be made in God's image. In this chapter, we will map out some of the problems associated with different views of the imago Dei, highlighting some of the questions that arise from particular perspectives. In the following chapter, I go on to summarize a few contemporary perspectives with a view to understanding how they attempt to address some of the issues raised here. It is not my intention to supply answers to all these questions.

Many will be left unresolved because this is how they remain within contemporary scholarship. In many ways, this in itself speaks of a deeper truth: we cannot resolve all the questions surrounding the imago Dei, and there will always be some element of the unknowable in relation to this topic.

THE FALL AND THE LOST IMAGE

A number of questions surround the idea of whether (and if so, how) the image is lost in fallen humanity. This is not something that is directly addressed through the Scriptures; we are not told explicitly in what way the image of God in man and woman was affected by the fall. We know that man and woman were expelled from the garden and should now expect to die. What we do see is that in the beginning human beings are together with each other and with God, naked and unashamed. After they have transgressed and broken the one commandment they have been given by God, they hide from him. They are now naked and ashamed.

Having disobeyed God's one command, not to eat the fruit of the tree of the knowledge of good and evil, man and woman fall under a cursed existence. Their erstwhile harmonious relationship with God and with each other is now characterized by lies, shame, pain, hardship, and toil. Furthermore, their harmonious relationship with the creation is also marred. One of the consequences of their disobedience is not that they die immediately having broken the commandment, but that they become mortal. Eventually they will die, as God warned them. In Gen 3:23, God says, "See, the man has become like one of us, knowing good and evil; and now, he might reach out his hand and take also from the tree of life, and eat, and live forever." What happens next in the story is that God prevents this.

The question of what constitutes precisely the sin of Adam and Eve is complex and invites multiple answers. We cannot discuss the nature of the first sin or sins here in detail. Similarly, however, interpretations of how God responds to the couple once they have sinned are also debated, and God's response to the couple has some bearing on how we understand the imago Dei. Where theologians are in some radical disagreement is over the question of the consequences of the fall, but naturally how we view this determines how we understand humanity's ongoing relationship with God postfall. Some see the banishment from the garden primarily as a punishment leading to a separation between humanity and God, and even as a form of rejection of humanity by God. Others see the fall in a different light, as a necessary point of growth and maturity as human beings learn to take responsibility and oversight of their world. Failure in this sense is not catastrophic, but a step toward maturity.[1] Still others see the consequences of the fall as God's mercy in the midst of humanity's rebellion seen in the first couple's determination to follow their own path. I find the third option the most compelling.

First then, it is common to hear people say that sin separates us from God. This, however, is not what we see in Gen 3. The first humans try to hide from God, but they cannot. He does, of course, know where they are! God seeks them out and warns them of all they have brought upon themselves, but even then, he clothes them to hide their shame. It seems as though there are shades of punishment here, but there is a greater sense in which the couple now must pay a forfeit for their transgression in living with the consequences of their sin. The life they had enjoyed of constant communion with God and harmonious relationship

1. Gordon McConville cites Schüle, "Made in the 'Image of God'"; and Beckerleg, "'Image of God' in Eden," in McConville, *Being Human in God's World*, 36.

with one another and creation is shattered by their own act of willing disobedience, which they had already been warned would have disastrous consequences. However, God's mercy and compassion is clearly evident in the midst of this "manmade" catastrophe.

After Adam and Eve's eyes have been opened to the knowledge of good and evil, God limits their life span and thus to some extent curbs their power on earth. Moreover, although they have to live with the consequences of their sin, they are not abandoned. God follows them out of the garden and goes with them into the world. He remains as close as possible to Cain, warning him not to murder his brother, but to no avail. And still, despite continuing hard-heartedness and rebellion, humanity is not abandoned or separated from God. God's response, instead, is to form covenants with human beings, revealing those covenants to individuals (Noah, Abraham, Moses, and David). God makes promises to humanity that God then binds himself to even if and when his covenant partners prove unfaithful, which inevitably they do. The greatest of these covenants is made in Christ through the sacrifice of the Son on the cross, through which forgiveness and restoration is then offered to all humanity. The story of human beings made in the image of God is that even when we are not godlike in any way, and perhaps especially then, God is still *for us*.

However we think about the image of God before the fall, being made in God's image clearly did not mean that Adam and Eve were fully like God or godlike at creation; had they been, they could not and would not have transgressed as they did in the first place. That they were made in God's image was not a statement about their perfection per se. Given this, it is hard to make a definitive statement as to the presence or absence of the image after the fall. What did the first couple have that they lost in the expulsion from the garden? Whatever we believe about a vestigial image of God, there is no doubt that the fall signals a loss of something, but a loss of what? The answers to this question are multilayered—and again, we do not have the answers spelled out to us in the Scriptures. As a result, theologians piece together what this fall means for humanity. Whatever or wherever we perceive the image to be in the first place will, to some extent, determine whether we think the image was lost in the fall, how we think this happened, and where we see the consequences of that in the world.

Throughout Genesis and beyond into the ongoing story of God's people, we see the consequences of human rebellion against God: murder, war, rape, greed, oppression of the poor and of women, tribal and ethnic hostility, lies, shame, and pain. As we have seen, this new existence does not signal a loss of God's presence, as God goes with man and woman out of the garden and continues to dwell with his people. However, life after the fall does seem as though it is a loss of God being present to them in a particular way. Just as there is hostility between men and women, brothers and sisters, parents and children, so the relationship of humanity to God is marked by rebellion and disobedience from humanity's side and thus is marred and fractured. The ongoing and unbroken peace between God and humans has departed. Secondly, after the fall Adam and Eve do not suffer an immediate loss of life; indeed, they are very much alive, and yet it seems as though they become mortal when they were not before. Dwelling with God for eternity is lost and delayed for a time to come. In this in-between time, death is experienced by humans mostly as a devastating rupture and loss.

Thirdly, the fall does not signal a complete loss of power or dominion as human beings continue to wield power in this world and still dominate the planet in multifarious ways. Again though, the relation of humanity to creation is marred and disrupted by sin; creation suffers through the greed and rapaciousness of human beings. The apostle Paul seems to have received some revelation that the creation itself is groaning as in the pains of childbirth, longing for the adoption of the sons of God. Somehow, the redemption of human bodies will signal the redemption of the whole earth (Rom 8:19–23). In the meantime, the dominion of human beings on this planet is marked by struggle and disharmony. Thus, even though human beings remain a powerful and, in some ways, the most powerful force on the planet, we still lack the ability to control natural forces, including disease and natural disasters that destroy what we build. We see great evidence of this all around us. Thus, we see both a loss of human capacity to steward and control as well as the loss of human capacity to do this well. Furthermore, as a result of sin, human beings can even play a demonic role in relation to one another and creation. Where is the image in all of this? Here theologians are divided.

Augustine held to the idea that a vestige of the image remained in fallen human beings: "And therefore if it is with reference to its capacity to use reason and understanding in order to understand and gaze upon God that it was made to the image of God, it follows that from the moment this great and wonderful nature begins to be, this image is always there, whether it is so worn away as to be almost nothing, or faint and distorted, or clear and beautiful."[2] Thomas Aquinas follows Augustine in this, claiming that the image is restored to be both clear and beautiful in the case of the just.[3] Some, not all, Reformers believed the image to have been obliterated. Others believed a trace of the image remained in humanity but was so distorted as

2. Augustine, *On the Trinity* 14.2.6.

3. Aquinas, *Summa Theologica* 1.93.8 ad. 3.

to have been to all intents and purposes annihilated. There are those, however, in other traditions who believe that the image of God resides in all humanity as some kind of inner light, serving as a connecting point to the divine, and as a source of goodness regardless of sin. The greatest schism, therefore, is between the idea (on the one hand) that the image has been totally obliterated by sin, and (on the other) that there is a light in all humanity that gives a capacity for goodness and truth and bestows the ability to apprehend the divine. Is humanity fundamentally disconnected from God because of the loss of the image, or fundamentally connected to God through possessing the image?

Historically, this debate has raged over the question of the relation of nature and grace. It is not possible here to outline the extent of the debate, but broadly there is a sharp divide between Roman Catholic and Protestant perspectives on the relationship of nature to grace, and this debate impinges on the doctrine of the imago Dei. Without wishing to be too sweeping, we can say that Protestantism sees a fundamental hiatus or discontinuity between nature and grace whereas Roman Catholicism sees an unbroken connection or continuity. For Protestants, that which human beings are in their natural state through sin means that they are no longer able to reach toward God. Our natures are so corrupt that we cannot save ourselves, and we need something external to ourselves—the grace of God in Christ—to break in and to rescue and redeem us. Within Roman Catholic thought, there is no such hiatus. Following Thomas Aquinas, Roman Catholics assert that grace perfects or heals the nature within. Hence, instead of a discontinuity, there is a fundamental continuity between nature and grace, characterized by an intrinsic, not an extrinsic, move of God within a person. This harks back to the difference between the optimistic view of human nature that we see in Renaissance humanists, and the pessimistic view of human nature we see in the Reformers.

Conor Cunningham provides an explanation of the Roman Catholic perspective in which he rejects dualism in its many forms. To some extent, this seems to capture the spirit of the age, as we will go on to see in Chapter 5. In a short presentation on nature and grace, Cunningham claims that this topic is of interest not just to theologians but touches the very heart of all existence because it is about who we are as human beings and how we relate to God. With respect to these questions around nature and grace, he comes out in the strongest possible terms against dualism. In his view, the human being is not a composite of body and soul, but one entity: the soul does not exist without the body, because the soul is an embodied person. "You don't *have* a soul," he claims, "you *are* a soul." And this soul is who you are—body and spirit. This physicalist view of the image places a great emphasis on the incarnation. Cunningham goes on, "God sends his Son into [the earth] to perfect it, not to destroy, not to subsume it, or moralize it, not to spiritualize it, but to make it more physical."[4] Thus, we see the fundamental continuity characteristic of modern Roman Catholic thought. The sense of continuity we see in Cunningham's thought is also a characteristic of an Eastern Orthodox perspective on God's interaction with the world, although an Eastern account would place the emphasis on theosis or divinization of humanity, whereas Cunningham's emphasis lies on the natural world becoming more creaturely, as it were.

Having said all this, most orthodox Christians would agree that whatever route we take, the image is fully restored only in Christ. We will continue to explore other disputed issues and problems associated with various perspectives.

4. Cunningham, "Why Study Nature and Grace? with Conor Cunningham."

THE IMAGE AND THE RATIONAL MIND

A number of criticisms are leveled at substantialist accounts of the imago Dei, and I think it would be fair to say these accounts have largely fallen out of favor in the contemporary world. Much of the reason they have fallen out of favor is linked to what we see in Cunningham's perspective above. Firstly, many critics claim that substantialist accounts focus solely on the intellectual aspects of existence and are therefore dualistic, overly cerebral, and incapable of accommodating the earthiness of embodied existence. Secondly, they do not rest on a faithful exposition of Gen 1 and 2, as they fail to take into account the calling on humanity to rule and reign, and the functional aspects therein. The third critique questions whether we are able to locate a human faculty or attribute we share with God that is applicable to all human beings in all states of existence. Can we say with certainty what human beings possess now or possessed before the fall (depending on our view of the postfall image) that makes them godlike? Moreover, if the image is understood in terms of intellectual capacity, then by default we will be excluding all manner of human beings with various intellectual or cognitive impairments.

The fourth critique is that substantialist accounts are predicated on the idea that this godlike faculty is one that differentiates us from nonanthropic creatures on the basis that human beings are unique in creation. However, the more we discover of nonanthropic creatures, the harder it is to establish which specific faculty human beings possess that animals do not. As Bruce McCormack has remarked, the doctrine of the imago Dei understood in this way has been "made to answer the wrong questions," viz. what makes us like God and what makes us different from animals?[5]

5. McCormack, "Panel Discussion at Los Angeles Theology Conference, 2015."

A further problem with substantialist accounts is that they are essentially epistemological, predicated on the idea that the image is linked to the *knowledge* of God in some way. As a corollary of this, it is often implied that this knowledge grows over time as reflected in a person's increasing closeness to God, in a person's sanctification, or both. There are a number of problems with this view. The first is a growing recognition that a life of discipleship is not necessarily a steady, upward ascent toward God, but is marked by constant ups and downs, failures (sometimes more as we grow older), and stumbling blocks. In addition to this, there is also a growing awareness (a) of people who lack certain cognitive abilities and (b) that many people face a deterioration of their cognitive abilities, degenerative illnesses, and just a weakening of all faculties—which means that we do not witness a growing knowledge of God as such. The substantialist view is questioned when it seems to imply that we might both identify and somehow measure the presence of the image within a person. Sheila Briggs writes, from a feminist perspective, that there "has been a shift in the interpretation of the doctrine of the imago Dei away from the divine image residing in human cognitive abilities or in the human distinction from other animals to the divine image as the foundation and guarantor of human dignity."[6] As we will see in Chapter 5, however, the substantialist view still has some value in certain forms.

KINGSHIP, PRIESTHOOD, AND STEWARDSHIP

As we have already noted, there are a number of difficulties with royal imagery in that it depicts human beings (and potentially only Christians) as superior beings on the earth. This is problematic on a number of counts. Firstly, it is quite

---

6. Briggs, "What is Feminist Theology?," 75.

clear that human beings are the cause of the majority of suffering on the earth and have been throughout history, so it is hard to make a case for the idea that humanity might have a unique role to play in the purification, healing, and just rule of the earth. Secondly, it is nigh on impossible to evacuate ideas of imperialism, hierarchy, dominant rule, and unequal power relations from the language of kingship and royalty. In order to counteract this, those who advocate royalty and kingship as the primary lens through which to understand the image often assert that this language should be understood through the servant paradigm that we see in Christ. The ruling and imperialist overtones are ameliorated by understanding kingship in relation to Christ, who came to serve and not to be served, and whose kingship leads him to the cross. The christological interpretation is a compelling argument, but the point about how this might be corrupted in the hands of human beings also stands.

For this reason, some see priesthood as a better paradigm, denoting more naturally, as it does, the kind of servant and mediatorial role lacking in kingship. This is a fair point, and priesthood imagery is an attractive option, although on its own it seems to exclude a number of other references in Scripture to the image. As many point out, priesthood is a cultic and not a family image, and given the history of the celibate priesthood, this paradigm is obviously not associated with the command in Gen 1:28 to be fruitful and multiply. In addition to this, the history of the priesthood in the church has led many to associate this image also with unequal power relations and abuse. These are some of the reasons that many are now turning to the language of stewardship and responsibility, of care and nurture, rather than rule and reign. This language, they believe, has enshrined within it the requisite humility needed, given the terrible history of humankind on the planet, and communicates the relation between humanity and the earth. Questions remain, however, about how effectively the people of God carry out any of the roles central to these paradigms, and indeed questions persist about whether all humanity is called to play a part in bearing the divine image.

Functional perspectives of the image, like substantialist perspectives are, of course, anthropocentric, but are also idealistic and teleological. In other words, they are founded on ideal conceptions of the role of humanity on the earth, and they are shaped by the idea that the rule, reign, stewardship, and priesthood of humanity has not yet come into being in any full sense of that. We are still waiting for this to be fulfilled. There is no denying the fact that the godlike rule, reign, priesthood, service, or stewardship of humanity on the earth is still in a very mixed form, as human beings are neither godlike rulers nor godly priests and stewards. This depiction of humanity appears, on balance, to be more anticipatory, prescriptive, and prophetic than descriptive and concrete.

Thus, the question to the functional view is, in what way is the image instantiated in the here and now. We cannot claim that the people of God perfectly represent him on this earth, or that they willingly carry out his will. Human beings are far from being unadulterated conduits of truth, beauty, and goodness, or channels of blessing to the world. Hence, we see a similar type of critique made against the functional view as we see against the substantialist view in relation to human capacity. With such an emphasis on praxis and the image lived out in active service to God, does this exclude those who cannot, for some reason, participate in this kind of service? If so, how do we navigate this, and what answers do we provide to these questions?

TELEOLOGICAL, THEOCENTRIC, AND EXTRINSIC MODELS

Peter Comensoli addresses the question of how a particular perspective of the image might relate to the profoundly intellectually impaired and is thus critical of what he calls all teleological, theocentric, and extrinsic models of the imago Dei.[7] As we have seen, a teleological perspective of the image is by necessity both promissory and deferred. It is predicated on the idea that the fulfilment of the image is yet to come. Comensoli's concern with this is that these views have little to say about who or what we are now. He proposes that any theology of the imago Dei should recognize the profoundly impaired as persons "in virtue of the lives they are living" and not on the basis of something that they may become.[8] Comensoli's point is one about where we locate the *worth* of a human life through our doctrine of the imago Dei.

For similar reasons, therefore, Comensoli also rejects purely theocentric models, where the image does not really reside within the person, but eternally resides in God. This is probably a trait of some Reformed, christocentric perspectives of the image where the image is borrowed, as it were, by humanity, but never possessed. Comensoli argues that theocentric views of the image ground the worth of human beings elsewhere—in the unconditional love of God, but not in the person.[9] And finally, he also targets extrinsic models such as friendship, claiming that the image of God is shaped by the notion of a friendship conferred over and against innate personhood.[10] In response, Comensoli him-

---

7. Comensoli, *In God's Image*, 55.

8. Comensoli, *In God's Image*, 11.

9. Comensoli, *In God's Image*, 37.

10. Comensoli, *In God's Image*, 53.

self takes a Thomist perspective in order to argue for the innate worth of a human being, which we will return to in Chapter 5.

Further questions surrounding relational models pertain to whether we understand them in terms of the need for both parties to acknowledge and to participate in the relationship. Given that all relational models are predicated on reciprocal relationships, and given that we normally understand those relationships to be characterized by mutual acknowledgement, the models raise questions about what forms that acknowledgement and reciprocity take, and whether these forms are applicable to all people. Do human beings need to understand themselves as being in a relationship with God for the image to be realized? How much and in what way are human beings called to respond in order for the image to be formed within? How does this relate to those who either do not wish to or cannot respond in any recognizable fashion? In many ways, the challenges posed to the relational models, like challenges to the other models, are raised by the question of impairment and disability, but there are also questions pertaining to how our doctrine of the imago Dei relates to those who are not in a recognizable relationship with God at all. What claims are we making about their status as the image? To some extent, this can be addressed if we make a distinction between active and passive participation, with God as the sole actor and humanity as the recipient of the conferred relationship, but this does not resolve all the questions.

AN INCLUSIVE IMAGE

We noted that in previous centuries, there were assumptions functioning in relation to the imago Dei that fueled particular exclusive views that prioritized the White, able-bodied

European male. To some extent, contemporary critiques arise from a general trend within our society to recognize the full personhood and rights of those who do not conform to this stereotype, and this is a welcome corrective. This challenge is now coming from numerous quarters, some of which we will consider in the following chapter. What we see in postmodern Western society is a marked shift toward, not just a toleration of diversity and a recognition of pluralism, but a call to respect and even celebrate difference. This has had an impact on Christian doctrine. In addition to this, there is a call for the doctrine of the imago Dei to be rooted in real lives and concrete existence rather than in some kind of idealized human being, relationship, or set of conditions of life. Contemporary accounts of the imago are concerned with explaining how the image might be present in diverse, varied, frail, and vulnerable minds, bodies, and lives. We will come back to these critiques and some of the solutions offered in contemporary theology in Chapter 5, but for now will focus on one of the central critiques leveled at theologies of the image: the criticism that for a very long time the image of God in humanity has been depicted in exclusively male terms.

WOMEN AND THE MALE IMAGE

The obvious androcentrism of the scriptural depictions of the image of God is hard to ignore, and this has given rise to numerous critiques of how we work out our theology of the image of God in light of the androcentrism of the Christian faith. The primary foundations for androcentrism in relation to the image lie first in the Genesis texts, with the primacy of Adam; then in the maleness of Christ; and lastly in 1 Cor 11:7–9, where the apostle Paul apparently identifies the male as the one who reflects the image and glory of God, whereas woman is simply the glory of man. The problem of an androcentric doctrine of the imago Dei is further compounded by our masculine pronouns for God, by language of kingship, which is exclusively male, and by language of priesthood, which for many centuries has also been exclusively male.

In the first place, there is an ongoing debate as to whether the Genesis narratives actually do lead us to the conclusion that God created the world around the primacy of the male. Secondly, if we do think they do, there is further debate as to whether this is because it was God's intention to accord a greater authority to men over women and children, or whether the dominance of men in the form of patriarchy is, in fact, a result of the fall. Despite the reference to the male and the female made in the image and likeness of God in Gen 1:27 (where it appears that man and woman are created completely equal), the account in Gen 2 leads many to claim that as the man was made first and the woman second, this precedence indicates that the man is placed in an authoritative position in creation, and that woman is to be in submission. This view is bolstered by a reading of Paul's letters whereby it is claimed, for example, that the theology of Eph 5, 1 Tim 2, and 1 Cor 11 endorses this hierarchicalist view, even though Gen 3:16 presents men's rule over women as one of the dire consequences of the fall. Tragically, the hierarchalist view has been powerful throughout Christian history and continues to hold sway in many churches and denominations throughout the world. However, throughout church history, there has also always been evidence of some resistance to the hierarchalist readings of these texts, as the texts themselves are actually ambivalent about equality and can be read to endorse equality rather than hierarchy between men and women. We will return to this in Chapter 5.

SEX, GENDER, AND SEXUALITY

A further challenge to the image as male and female, however we understand this claim, is now coming from a postmodern view that both gender and even biological sex should no longer be viewed in the binary terms of male and female. Sex is normally differentiated from gender in that the sex of a person is deemed to be determined by their biological make up and their reproductive organs while gender is normally understood to refer to the psychological, behavioral, social, and cultural aspects of maleness or femaleness. Sexuality normally refers to how one expresses sexual attraction and who or what one finds sexually attractive. In contemporary thought, however, there are a number of differing opinions as to how sex is related to gender and vice versa, and how both of these are related to sexuality. Confusingly, *sex* and *gender* are currently terms that are often used interchangeably in common parlance without much precision.

In relation to a person's sex, there are those who now argue that biological sex is not determinative of whether a person is male or female but that these concepts (man/woman and male/female) now lie in an individual's perception of what they believe themselves to be. Hence, a transgender person with male reproductive organs may tell those around them that they are in fact a woman, and require others around them to acknowledge this. The same is true of a transgender person with female reproductive organs who may tell others they are a man. In addition to this there are those who identify themselves as non-binary in relation to male and female meaning they see themselves as neither one nor the other. Transgender and non-binary people are not to be confused with intersex people, who are born with both male and female reproductive organs.

When doctors became able to operate on a person to change their reproductive organs, parents of intersex children were coerced into making a decision about which sex their child should be before the child could choose for themselves what they wanted to do. That a choice was made for a person has proven to be enormously damaging for individuals who underwent these procedures. Thankfully, this has now changed, and, for the most part, children are allowed to grow up as intersex people without being forced to choose, although there is much more work to be done on understanding the phenomenon of intersex.[11]

In relation to gender, there are now numerous categories denoted by LGBTQI+. Again, this is somewhat confusing, and some of the terms refer to gender and others to sexuality. The categories are not that clear. What is clear in the postmodern West is that sex, gender, and sexuality are all categories that are defined by a form of hypersubjectivity, and any external judgment that questions a person's subjective description of themselves is viewed as oppression. Gender is seen as fluid whereas sexuality can be either fluid or fixed, depending on the individual's perception of their preferences. Interestingly, many people (even the most liberal) still refer to character traits with the binary terms *male* and *female* or *masculine* or *feminine*, whereas the Bible is silent on this issue. There are no descriptions of essentialized masculinity or femininity in the Scriptures.

All these issues raise questions with respect to how we understand the image in relation to the body, and there are no easy answers to these questions—especially as bodies are now viewed by many as essentially editable to conform to how we see ourselves in our own minds. We can change who and what we are on request, or we can simply

11. See DeFranza, "Journeying from the Bible to Christian Ethics," for more on this issue.

pronounce that though we appear to be one thing, we are, in fact, another, because our inner beings (psyche, emotion, spirit) tell us what and who we are. We will revisit some of these questions in Chapter 5. In this chapter, we have simply raised some of the common objections to different perspectives on the imago Dei in order to highlight the difficulty in claiming that one view might provide a comprehensive picture for all cultures in all times and circumstances.

DISCUSSION QUESTIONS

1. Have you been under the impression that sin separates us from God? What are some of the problems associated with this view?

2. What do you understand as some of the aspects of the fall in relation to the imago Dei?

3. Having read about some of the problems associated with different views of the imago Dei, which version do you still find most compelling?

4. What might be some of the advantages and disadvantages associated with rooting the imago Dei in lives that we live now rather than in some kind of ideal?

5

MODERN PERSPECTIVES I

INTRODUCTION

IT IS NOT POSSIBLE in such a brief volume to do justice to the plethora of modern perspectives on the doctrine of the image of God. In addition, as I have noted throughout, this doctrine is one that will be constantly evolving as people revise their understandings of personhood, relationship, existence, the role of humanity in creation, and other topics. In this chapter, therefore, I simply summarize a few different proposals in order to provide a picture of the range of thinking on this topic and to point readers to some contemporary perspectives.

Many contemporary Western viewpoints have in common a number of traits—traits that differentiate them from many traditional perspectives on the image of God, and traits that reflect, I believe, times in which we live. The first is the claim that the doctrine of the image of God should be defined in relation to life as it is lived now, taking into account the conditions of existence, and not solely a doctrine that applies to a future, heavenly sphere. The second characteristic, associated with the first claim, is that the doctrine should be broad enough to include the whole of humanity in all its diversity as well as in all its states of being. The third is that we should acknowledge the significance of the body; and importantly, the body as it is and not as an idealized archetype. This means the idea of our physical existence has come to the fore—who we are in our bodies (including our physical appearance, our skin color, our abilities and our capabilities) matters. All these have something to contribute to our understanding of what it means to be the image. This signals quite a radical shift in thinking. Instead of beginning with some kind of idea of a perfect image (however we might imagine that) and working our way back to human being as it is now, thinking is going in the other direction. It is, as it were, a theological anthropology from below. Theologians are beginning with the images we have in front of us in ourselves and in one another and reasoning towards a theology of the image from there. There is a move, therefore, away from teleological, perfectionist, flawless, static, homogeneous, and overly cerebral accounts of the imago toward the idea that the doctrine should also account for our reality, our diversity, and our bodily existence. This move signals a shift away from universals to particulars, and a recognition of the diversity of human nature. It is also, I suggest, associated with a general trend in academia whereby experience is now admitted as a valid epistemological category. In other words, if how we experience life is judged to be a valid measure of what is true and real, then experience must be taken into account in formulating existential questions and answers. This admits new concepts to the conversation.

In the following two chapters, I offer a range of views and perspectives. Some undertake a retrieval of ancient perspectives to aid us in our thinking on this topic. Others advocate viewing the image in dynamic and performative terms, as a verb rather than a noun. There are those who see the image in terms of identity, those who argue that our sexuality and sexual desire needs to be taken into account in relation to the image, and as a sign of the times there are also those who are asking questions around the image of God in relation to transhumanism and all that that entails.

THE LENS OF EMBODIMENT

Throughout church history, we can trace a general tendency to portray the body with its carnal desires in a negative light, as something to tame, repress, or escape from. This is not true of all theologies everywhere, of course, but it has been a dominant theme in the West. A move away from this to theologies of embodiment, therefore, is significant. However, it is not only that desire (especially sexual desire) has often been painted in a negative light in previous centuries. The main reason behind the hesitancy to focus on bodily existence as the image of God is the problematic relationship of bodily existence to God, whose essence is disembodied. Hence, if we are thinking along the lines of how a human person is made in God's image, the body is not the first aspect of the person that we might cite, as God is neither embodied nor gendered. In addition to this, anthropomorphizing tendencies in theology easily lead to us creating God in our own image rather than the other way round so we should be cautious in this regard. Having said that, however, it seems important not to consign the body to irrelevance but, somehow, to take our bodies into account.

Firstly, it is only in our embodied existence that we are ever confronted by the reality that I and another might be the image of God. Secondly, it is only in our bodies that we are able to image God one to another in any concrete fashion. Thirdly, through the incarnation, we see that when God chooses to reveal himself through the perfect image of God and humanity, he comes as a man in the flesh. As we have noted, Irenaeus stands out for acknowledging this connection between Christ's bodily existence and our own. We have also seen an example of this in the previous chapter, with Conor Cunningham's positive appraisal of the natural, material world. We live, love, rejoice, and suffer in our bodies. We become who we are in and through our bodies, and our bodies and how we experience them are part of how we are shaped as people. Moreover, our bodies will not be expunged, but renewed. It is these same bodies that we have lived with that will be resurrected to eternal life (1 Cor 15:53–54; Phil 3:21). So, it seems appropriate to speak of how the image is expressed through and in bodily terms in some way.

"TO IMAGE" GOD

Conceptualizing the image of God as a lived phenomenon, Alistair McFadyen argues that we should move away from static and essentialist definitions toward a more dynamic, interactive, and relational perspective.[1] Central to his argument is defining the imago Dei in relation to the doctrine of creation, but with a significantly different emphasis from that which we see in the functional view. McFadyen understands creation not as a one-off event, but as a "continuing and interactive movement of God relating to the world creatively."[2] To this end, he advocates understanding the image of God in terms of a verb rather than a noun—to image God. McFadyen's account is a good example of how an appreciation of the exigences of existence are driving

---

1. McFadyen, "Redeeming the Image."
2. McFadyen, "Redeeming the Image," 109.

theological reflection on the image. He explicitly states that we cannot proceed as though humanity were a "fixed, known or even knowable datum, a conceptual deposit retrievable from God's original act of creation awaiting more adequate description or abstraction of universal, defining properties. Rather, humanity is more of a quality to be sought and worked out in the contingencies of concrete situations."[3] As a result, McFadyen cautions against definitions of the image that "so spiritualize, moralize, or otherwise etherealize it that the material base of our creatureliness and therefore our dependence on and commonality with the rest of creation are thereby threatened."[4] The body, therefore, has significance. More than this, McFadyen develops his image theology in relation to suffering bodies in particular and reflects upon how human beings might be able to enact what it means to be the image of God in particular contexts where men and women need redemption.

Thus, in his view, we should be seeking definitions that are not so much "definitive or taxonomic as performative, working out what it might mean 'to image God.'"[5] This propels McFadyen toward focusing on particular situations where human beings "cry out" to God for deliverance out of deep distress, and where humanity has been "denigrated, damaged, denied, distorted, disoriented, limited."[6] He applies this to Black theology, feminist theology, and post 9/11 theological discussions of torture. This is clearly far more specific in its focus than we have seen in other accounts and more developed toward suffering and justice than we have encountered previously even though accounts of the image in terms of the development of Christian love

---

3. McFadyen, "Redeeming the Image," 111.
4. McFadyen, "Imaging God," 921.
5. McFadyen, "Redeeming the Image," 112.
6. McFadyen, "Redeeming the Image," 111.

and charity sow the seeds for this kind of perspective. It is the specificity of the application of image theology here that characterizes postmodern accounts. This gives more scope for developing the doctrine of the image in the light of diverse human lives.

DIVERSITY

One of the serious problems we encountered in relation to the doctrine of the image of God was the distortion of image theology within a European patriarchal and colonial culture. It is clear to see how the doctrine of the image of God has been tainted by exceptionalism, hegemony, privilege, and the belief of the superiority of White people over others. The idea that a White European man is a superior version of the image of God over women and Black and Brown people has dominated much of the thinking around the imago Dei with abhorrent effects.

Soong Chan Rah names this as "the sin of racism," where "Western Christianity took this doctrine [of the imago Dei], which affirms the dignity of every human being, and warped it to elevate one people group over another."[7] Many cite the use of what is called "the curse of Ham" to justify the abuse and oppression of Black men and women that we particularly see through the trans-Atlantic slave trade, but that is also evident in other histories and even to the present day. The idea of the curse of Ham is based on a distorted account from Scripture, but the narrative is worth recounting. In Gen 9:20–27 is a story of Ham, the son of Noah, who is cursed by his father for a heinous breach of propriety, the nature of which we cannot fully fathom. One day, Ham sees his father asleep, drunk, and naked, but rather than covering him and never speaking of it (which one

7. Rah, "The Sin of Racism," 207.

imagines is what he should have done), he tells his brothers, Shem and Japheth, what he saw. The brothers go straight-away and cover their father, being careful not to look on his nakedness all the while. When Noah awakes, he discovers what Ham has done, presumably because his brothers told their father, and for this Ham is cursed with being enslaved to his brothers. The story never mentions skin color, and clearly the brothers were all of the same heritage anyway, so there is seemingly no scope for differentiating between Ham's skin color and his brothers' skin color. Horrifyingly, however, in centuries to come, Ham and his descendants were identified as Black by Christians, Muslims, and Jews, and the "curse of Ham" was used by many to justify the en-slavement of Black people. The fabricated narrative of the curse of Ham justified the enslavement, torture, desecra-tion, defilement, and murder of the African people.

It is no wonder then that this distortion is being cor-rected in contemporary thinking. The focus on embodi-ment aids us in this task, as it leads us toward understanding that a human being is the person they are in their own body with its own color, shape, sex, and so forth: it is in *this* body that this person represents the image of God. Such a focus on embodiment allows us to celebrate the diversity of the human race rather than to attempt to subsume diversity under an idealized, otherworldly, or purely spiritual version of the image of God. Emphasizing the diversity of cultural formation, Willie James Jennings rejects a hegemonic con-ceptualization of the image of God, rooting the doctrine instead in the earthly conditions that shape us and mold us to be the people that we are now.[8] Like Peter Comensoli, Jennings rejects extrinsic views of the image. Rather, he ar-gues, the image is instantiated in human beings as they are, and furthermore this specificity and diversity will endure

8. See Jennings, *The Christian Imagination*.

in the eschaton rather than be erased by a sea of uniformity. This perspective, expressed so well in Jennings's work, can be found in Black, Asian, Latinx, feminist, womanist, mujerista and queer theologies, as well as in those articulating theologies of the image in relation to disability. These contemporary theologies signal both a dismantling of idealistic notions of the body and a decentring of White, male perspectives as universal concepts of the image.

That the distortions of imago Dei theology have been largely male-dominated is clearly evident. However, it is also evident that White women have participated in and been beneficiaries of the privileges of Western supremacy in ways that Black and Brown women have not and are not—hence the need for specific theologies from female Black and Brown theologians. There are specific issues in relation to Black women that womanist theologians emphasize (routinely in negative terms), including the denigration of Black women in White, Western culture. Multiple womanist scholars could be referenced here. One in particular, Phyllis Sheppard, writes from a psychoanalytical perspective, identifying the process of sexualization, projection, and disavowal that goes on in relation to how Black women's bodies are perceived in White, Western culture, while the beauty of Black women's bodies is denied.[9] The result of this is that the other is both kept as other while also kept in submission. This same principle could be applied to other people groups such as Asian or Latina women. The point here is to establish a divide between one group and another in order to claim that one group, more than another, reflects the image of God. This has the effect, as history has

---

9. Sheppard, *Self, Culture, and Others*. For more on the horror of the abuse and torture of Black bodies, see Baptist, *The Half Has Never Been Told*.

shown, of othering and subjugating many people who are not in the privileged group.

The White, Western church has a chequered, sometimes shameful history—one that is only really being exposed as I write. There is much more work to be done in rewriting theologies of the image in relation to the diversity of the human race. It is not that many have not tried before to expose corrupt and abhorrent theology and practice within the church, but since the growing protests of 2020 associated with the Black Lives Matter movement, the sin of racism has been harder to ignore. Theology has a part to play in destroying lies and speaking out about the truth of the value and equality of all members of the human race; clearly, image-of-God theology plays a crucial role in this. In this vein, Rah, with Jennings, sees theology as having the "capacity to redefine the social" and as offering "the possibility of a prophetic imagination that can transform individuals and society."[10]

WOMEN AND THE IMAGE

We have touched on the question of how both patricentrism (father-centeredness) and androcentrism (masculine-centeredness) affect the idea that women are made in the image of God, and it is not as if there are not seeds of inequality sown in the Scriptures that can readily be exploited by those who wish to argue that the male of the species holds a privileged position in relation to God. As well as the androcentrism and patricentrism embedded in the Judaeo-Christian tradition, we have a creation story in Gen 2 in which the man is made first and woman is made for him, we have a male Saviour, and we have texts such as 1 Cor 11:7–9—all of which contribute to the idea that

10. Rah, "The Sin of Racism," 206.

somehow the male of the species reflects the image of God in a stronger or purer way than the female. Man takes precedence over woman. And as Mary Daly famously wrote, "If God is male then the male is God."[11] It is no wonder that patriarchy has dominated the church for centuries.

The question of male and female together as the image of God is further complicated by how we understand what the divine image has to do with how male and female relate to each other. As we have already seen, Karl Barth argues strongly for the idea that the image is only completed by the complementary relation of male and female, particularly in marriage. The disturbing aspect of these claims, which Barth himself disputes, but that appears elsewhere in other accounts of the imago Dei, is the idea that the man is the complete image on his own whereas the woman is not. This view is very much influenced by the 1 Cor 11:7–9. We see this, for example, in Augustine: "The woman together with her own husband is the image of God, so that the whole substance may be one image; but when she is referred to separately in her quality of help-meet, which regards the woman herself alone, then she is not the image of God; but as regards to the man alone, he is the image of God as fully and completely as when the woman too is joined with him."[12] The ramifications of this theology for any woman are shockingly clear, but perhaps especially for unmarried women.

The second problem with respect to man and woman and the image of God is related to a hierarchical view of the Trinity extrapolated from the apostle Paul's writings, specifically 1 Cor 11:3. Paul's statement here—that Christ is the head of every man or every husband, that man is the head of woman or husband the head of wife, and that God

11. Daly, *Beyond God the Father*, 3.
12. Augustine, *On the Trinity* 12.3.10.

is the head of Christ—has led to some powerfully oppressive teaching and practices whereby men are seen as having authority over women, who themselves are called to submit to male authority. The thinking behind this begins with a hierarchical view of the Father/Son relation within the Trinity, with reference to the concept of the head. According to this view, the Father is seen to be in an authoritative position over the subordinate, obedient Son. This is then mapped onto male/female relations, and deeply affects theologies of gender. For example, this reading is also associated with Barth's view of the male as active and the female as passive. Hence, those who take a hierarchical view of male and female first claim that there is an eternal subordination within the Trinity of the Son to the Father. They next claim, based on 1 Cor 11:3 (and Eph 5 where the word "head" is used by Paul in relation to the husband), that a husband/man has a God-given role of authority over a wife/woman, reflecting the role of the Father toward the Son. The wife/woman stands in the position of both the submissive Son and the submissive church as Christ's body. The man takes up the role of the authoritative head, but still in submission to the Father and Christ. Yet this view is further complicated by those who claim that the husband/man actually reflects primarily the role of God the Father: husband/man reflects and role of God the Son solely when the Son assumes an authoritative role over the church; the husband/man does not reflect the Son's submission to the Father; wives/women alone reflect the Son's submission to the Father.

There is much confusion over the question of subordination within the Trinity and analogies between the Trinity and human beings. Yet all of it is unnecessary in the light of orthodox Christianity, where any hint of intra-Trinitarian subordination was ruled out as heretical by the early church fathers. In short, there is no eternal subordination of the

Son to the Father, as both are of one substance; thus, the analogy between the persons of the Trinity and human beings falls away. Despite the erroneous nature of this theology of gender and the image as well as the illogicality of the argumentation and method, these ideas have tragically dominated many churches for many centuries. Thankfully, in recent years there has been much work done in theology around questions of the male and the female in the image of God. This work has exposed the patriarchal and even misogynistic bias in thinking, which is good news for women and for men. Many scholars in recent years have turned their attention to this question and offer detailed and sophisticated arguments highlighting specifically where a male bias has affected the translation, interpretation, and application of key scriptural passages to portray women in a particular light or to construct a certain male-centred theology where there was not one in the first place. We are now able to see how simple translation corrections yield alternative narratives in favor of women, and often give an opposing perspective to the hierarchical and patriarchal views of years gone by. I will give just two examples here, and further reading at the end of the chapter.

Only two references in the Bible deal specifically with man and woman and the image, so we will turn to these. The first is Gen 1:26–27. In Gen 1:26, we read that God created *adam*, which, as many point out, is not "man" as in the male of the species, but is better rendered "humanity." The text is ambivalent here as to whether this creation is a single unit of male and female or whether this signifies the making of both male and female as two forms of human being. A literal translation of the Hebrew is "male and female he created 'him,'" *not* "male and female he created them." The singular pronoun sounds strange in English, however, and so it is translated in the plural: "male and female he created them." The Hebrew text has led many recent commentators to comment on the androgynous nature of the first human being (a human creature), who becomes two—male and female. Maryanne Cline Horowitz notes that in the Jewish readings of this text there is even a hermaphrodite tradition in relation to the first human, although this is not one that was picked up by the early church.[13] So first, we see from the Gen 1 text that the idea of the image of God as male and female is more complex than one whole male image to which another is added.

However, the man and woman who are created in Genesis are described in different ways as the story progresses, and we come across the second account of creation where the man and the woman are described differently, so that the two accounts together do give us a complex picture. One of the ways we see this is the terms that are used for male and female, man and woman. The words used for male and female in Gen 1:27 are *zakar* and *neqeba* respectively. These are symbolic terms connoting "the-one-who-has-a-tip" for the man and "the-one-who-is-perforated" for the woman. These terms then apparently refer to the fittingness of these two for sexual relations but are not repeated again. In Gen 2:4 when the one human person has become two, they become *ish* (man) and *ishah* (woman). It is not until further on in the narrative that the man is given the name Adam (meaning human from the earth) as a proper name, and the woman the name of Eve (meaning living one). These two creatures are now differentiated by sex, but they are still of the same substance. They are bone of bone and flesh of flesh. It becomes obvious that this is a much more nuanced picture of sequence and relation between the man and the woman of Gen 1 and 2 than we are sometimes led to believe. Those who eschew hierarchical readings of the

13. Horowitz, "The Image of God in Man," 186.

position of man to woman from the Genesis texts focus on the unitive nature of the man and the woman, which has a much stronger foundation in the text than does the division between the two, which comes only after the fall. Similarly, although it might appear that the man is made first and woman is made for him in Gen 2, this simplistic narrative is ambivalent. There is, it turns out, no explicit reference to specifically male predominance or precedence as the image of God in Genesis, and the unequal relationship between husband and wife, where the husband "rules over" the wife, is a disastrous consequence of the fall (Gen 3:16).

As we have already seen, the question of whether the male/female complementarity is essential to the reflection of the image of God in humanity or not is a further cause of division. Is man alone the image to which woman is added? One of the other key texts that contributes to this view is 1 Cor 11:7–9 where the apostle Paul writes, "For man is the image and glory of God and woman is the glory of man ." As we have seen, in a cursory reading, this seems clear enough but, in fact, raises some intractable difficulties of interpretation in the light of Gen 1:26–27 as well as other Pauline texts. For a start, the use of "image and glory" rather than "image and likeness" is strange, and the seeming exclusion of the woman from this status, highly problematic. Interestingly, from very early on, bishops rejected the implication that man was made in the image of God and woman was not. So despite Augustine's belief that woman needs man to complete her image (based on 1 Cor 11), he also writes on 1 Cor 11:7 that this "seems to exclude woman altogether from being the image of God, in contradiction both to Christian good sense and to the text of Gen 1:27."[14] Augustine has his own very complex reading of 1 Cor 11:7–9,

14. Augustine, *On the Trinity* 12.3, abstract.

which I have written about in more detail elsewhere.[15] Essentially he argues that men are associated with the rational mind and higher affairs whereby human beings are able to contemplate God, and women are associated with lower affairs and the carnal aspects of existence. He makes the point though that the distinctions the apostle Paul makes in 1 Cor 11:7–9 are solely symbolic and have nothing to do with any essential attributes in men and women.

The ancients in general, however, quite naturally held to the primacy of the male, and this prevails through many centuries up until today. Man is associated with the rational mind, authority, and leadership, and woman with a lesser ability to think, subordination, and following. Woman was deemed to have a helpmeet status and so is relegated to a lower order. For the most part, even when churchmen and theologians held to these patriarchal views, they would also argue that this does not mean that a woman is less of the image, although as we have seen, 1 Cor 11:2–16 creates enormous difficulties for anyone attempting to formulate a theology of gender, whether attempting to argue that woman should be subordinate to man or that woman and man are fully equal. Either position is difficult to demonstrate from the text itself, as the whole passage focuses on head coverings or hairstyle, telling us that Paul believed the Corinthian women should make up for something they lack in their own natures by attiring themselves in a particular way in the public assembly so as not to shame their heads: God, Christ, and the man.

There is no doubt that the theology and practices in 1 Cor 11 lead, not just to the idea that men and women are in some kind of complementary relationship, but in the direction of the woman as a lesser image. Thomas Aquinas writes this on 1 Cor 11:7:

15. Peppiatt, "Man as the Image."

> In its principal signification, male and female
> are both created in the image of God. In a sec-
> ondary sense the image of God is found in man,
> and not in woman: for man is the beginning
> and end of woman; as God is the beginning and
> end of every creature. So when the Apostle had
> said that *man is the image and glory of God, but
> woman is the glory of man*, he adds his reason for
> saying this: *For man is not of woman, but woman
> of man: and man was not created for woman, but
> woman for man.*[16]

There has been untold damage done to women by the
idea of the primacy of the male that can be gleaned from
1 Cor 11. The argument, however, rests on a Corinthian
gloss on Genesis rather than the other way around. Indeed,
a Genesis gloss on Corinthians leads us to the conclusion,
as Augustine and many others have pointed out, that Paul
is not explicating Genesis well. Colin Gunton's view of the
theology in 1 Cor 11:7–9 is that both Paul's exegesis and
theology are "questionable," whereas Michael Lakey states
more strongly that the theological and cultural codes within the passage are "aberrant and implausible."[17]

I have discussed this in great detail elsewhere, but in
summary, my view is that 1 Cor 11:7–9 reflects a Corinthian distortion of the creation story propagated by the
male leaders to keep the women quiet and in submission.[18]
As the entire weight of the scriptural data is in favor of the
equality of the image in man and woman, this should call
into question the Corinthian passage and not the other

16. Aquinas, *Summa Theologica* 1.93.4 ad. 1 (italics original to the
translation).

17. Gunton, "The Church on Earth," 69; Lakey, *Image and Glory*,
181.

18. For my full argument see Peppiatt, *Women and Worship at
Corinth.*

way around. Thus, in my view, 1 Cor 11:7 as a warrant for both the subordination of women and the need for them to cover their heads in the presence of men so deeply cuts across a canonical perspective on men and women that it is most likely this is an instance of Paul citing his opponents at Corinth. In addition to this, the idea that these views represent the Corinthian men's views fits very easily within a Stoic perspective that we would associate with Paul's largely Roman congregation and thus is an example of syncretism. However, even if this could be proved to be Paul's views and not a Corinthian citation, the difficulties with interpreting and applying this text to the modern day are so severe that we should probably admit that we cannot make sense of these verses for a contemporary context. The fact that the majority of churches in the world enforce neither head coverings for women nor certain hairstyles indicates that we have done just that! In the next chapter we turn to a few more contemporary debates in relation to the image.

DISCUSSION QUESTIONS

1. What possibilities open up for us in our thinking if we think of the image of God as a verb rather than a noun?

2. Have you considered the idea that the whole of humanity in all its diversity might image God?

3. Were you or was anyone you know under the impression that the male is a more perfect image of God than the female?

4. In what ways are you beginning to understand the imago Dei differently?

6

MODERN PERSPECTIVES II

SEX DIFFERENCE AND THE IMAGE

IN RECENT YEARS THERE have been a number of developments in relation to the ideas of sex difference and personhood that have had a profound impact on how people understand what it is to be male and female and how the two are related. This, in turn, will affect theologies of the image. There is a sense in which some of these questions around sex, gender, and sexuality are entirely new, and yet it is also true to say that some questions are not new. For example, theologians have always disagreed on the question of whether the sex difference of man and woman is essential to the image and if so, in what way. And as we have seen in Gregory of Nyssa, he rejects an essentialized view of sex and the image on the grounds that God is not a gendered being.[1] Similarly, Thomas Aquinas does not make much of the distinction of male and female in the creation story. "Therefore we must understand that when Scripture

1. Gregory of Nyssa, *On the Making of Man*, 16.8–9.

had said, *to the image of God he created him*, it added, *male and female he created them*, not to imply that the image of God came through the distinction of sex, but that the image of God belongs to both sexes, since it is in the mind, wherein there is no sexual distinction." Aquinas adds a reference to Gal 3:26–28 to back up his point. "Wherefore the Apostle . . . , after saying, *According to the image of Him that created him*, added, *Where there is neither male nor female*."[2] As we have noted in the previous chapter, the concept of the first human as essentially male from whom the second female human emerges is not as clear as some believe it to be. Neither is there any indication in the Genesis text that the image of God is only completed by the complementary relation of man and woman. Hence both of these popular conceptions in relation to man and woman and the image are problematic. We now turn to some more contemporary issues.

SEX, GENDER, AND SEXUALITY

As I mentioned briefly in Chapter 4, questions around sex, gender, and sexuality have taken on a particular emphasis in the contemporary West in recent years, which means there are currently unique challenges to the idea that human beings fall into binary categories in relation to both sex and gender. In past centuries, where the idea of human beings being identified as either male or female would have been completely unchallenged, we are undergoing a revolution in the West, where it is now common to hear people express the idea that a person's biological sex does not determine whether they are male and female. Consequently, sex and gender are deemed to be fluid rather than fixed. These are

2. Aquinas, *Summa Theologica* 1.93.6 ad. 2 (italics original to translation).

not views that are held unquestioningly by all people. It is probably true to say that these views are held most strongly among the liberal, educated elite and have, therefore, probably had more impact in academia and the teaching profession in general than anywhere else up to this point. It is also probably true to say that younger generations are more likely to accept the idea of the fluidity of sex and gender boundaries than are older people. Whether individuals hold entirely to the idea of the fluidity of sex and gender, in many spheres, this claim now goes unchallenged.

In theological academic terms, queer theology specifically represents a theological expression of a nonbinary worldview in which Scripture and tradition are viewed through the queering of the status quo and fixed boundaries, which results in new and often surprising and challenging perspectives. This hermeneutic is now placed alongside feminist theology, Black theology, Latinx theology, and a whole host of particular perspectives on God, the Bible, the church, and so forth.

The erasing of traditional boundaries raises interesting questions in relation to whether the male and female sex difference is in any way significant to image theology. One does not have to agree with the premise that there is no such thing as male or female, man or woman, masculinity or femininity, in order to see what theologies might arise out of this development. To some extent, we already see a version of this kind of thinking with Gregory, although he did not blur boundaries between male and female as such. With the blurring of the binary boundaries there are new ways of thinking about human being that can be taken in two opposing directions and give rise to quite different perspectives on the place of sex, gender, and sexuality in relation to the identity of the person.

Opposing Views

People tend to understand the concepts of sex, gender, and sexuality primarily either through the lens of immanence or of transcendence. An immanent view of sex, gender, and sexuality sees these as fixed attributes within a person and essential to their identity. A transcendent view understands sex, gender, and sexuality as contingent and not an essential aspect of personhood. For the most part postmodern views are essentially immanent, in that a person's chosen sex, gender, and sexuality is part of the core of their personhood, even if that is fluid. Moreover, it is expected that this immanent part of one's identity will be expressed in sexual relations. Again, what I am calling the immanent point of view on sex, gender, and sexuality tends to be assumed today whether one holds a traditional or progressive view on these matters. Traditionalists, for example, place a great weight on heterosexual marriage as a goal for all people, so in some that sense they see sex, gender, and sexuality as crucial to identity. Progressives, who are more likely to understand sex, gender, and sexuality as fluid, nevertheless believe that these qualities are core to human being and that a fulfilled life is one that is lived with sexual freedom.

Thus, whether one holds to the idea that one can change one's sex, gender, or sexual orientation, still the view that what we are or what we choose to be determines our very being is a premise that underlies both a conservative and a progressive perspective. The result is that many people in the West are inflexible, as it were, on the question of identity, but radically differ on the question of what constitutes a person's sex, gender, and sexuality and whether these are given or chosen. Furthermore, it is not only traditionalists who hold to the idea that sex, gender, and sexuality are given, so the boundaries between the fixedness and the fluidity of sex, gender, and sexuality fall in many different places depending on who one asks. It is important to note these cultural developments in a discussion on the image of God, but also worth noting that the conversation can be confusing, at times, to say the least. In addition to this, damage inflicted by rejection and even demonization of gay men and women, and by rejection and demonization of any minority (on the one hand), and gender politics around these subjects (on the other hand) mean that it is hard to conduct any form of dispassionate debate. Emotions run very high, and discussion is often freighted with pain and anger, which, although understandable, makes sharing and listening on the topic much harder.

Another perspective from a Christian view is the transcendent view of sex, gender, and sexuality, which is more ancient and not particularly in vogue, although there are those today who still advocate for this view. This is more in line with Gregory's perspective—that sex, gender, and sexuality (whatever we perceive this to be) is something that can be transcended. In other words, a person's sex, gender, and sexuality does not need to determine everything about their existence but can be risen above or sublimated through a new identity in Christ, this being the most dominant determinative factor of an individual's personhood and behavior. The transcendent view is seen most clearly in the celibate tradition, which dates back to the early church.

The tradition of forgoing marriage and sexual relations to focus attention on God classically allows men and women to define themselves not primarily in relation to one another in romantic or sexual relations, or primarily as sexual or even sexed beings, but as those who are in Christ and solely devoted to him. This is more in line with traditional Christian views associated with a body/soul or body/spirit dualism, but not a particularly popular view in postmodern Western Christianity. However, traditionally, a celibate lifestyle would have offered certain freedoms from labels and expectations that are attached to a particular sex, gender, or sexual orientation. For example, in years gone by a celibate life was seen to be a liberating life for women who did not wish to be defined by their relationship to a man, husband, brother, or father. This is not to say that in the transcendent view sex, gender, and sexuality disappear, but that they are no longer *the* defining features of who a person is and how they should lead their life. One of the negative aspects of the celibate tradition, however, has been the attempted repression of sexual desire, rather than the celebration of sexual desire as a good gift from God even if it is never acted upon. Much of what is discussed in contemporary debates stems from a recognition that sexual repression has not contributed to human flourishing.

THE REDEMPTION OF DESIRE

In relation to this last point there has been a further contemporary development, which is a move toward recognizing the goodness of human beings as sexual beings and redeeming erotic desire. This is taking shape through the number of theologians arguing for a redemptive view of sexuality. Again, this is not a new idea as such, as the language of erotic desire has always permeated certain strands of Christian mysticism. However, there is a sense in which this topic has come to the fore in recent years. Sarah Coakley is a proponent of these views, arguing for the redemption of the category of desire in our understanding of how we relate to the Trinitarian God.[3] In her view, human sexuality and spirituality are intertwined, and "the questions of right contemplation of God, right speech about God, and right

3. Coakley, *God, Sexuality, and the Self.*

ordering of desire all hang together."[4] Coakley explores the questions around intense human desire for God in contemplation, prayer, and worship in order to address the question of how we might think theologically about desire. First, she differentiates between desire and sex where the two are so often equated in the contemporary West. Second, she locates desire in God: "*desire is more fundamental than 'sex'.* It is more fundamental, ultimately, because desire is an ontological category belonging primarily to God, and only secondarily to humans as a token of their createdness 'in the image.'"[5] This understanding of human being includes desire as essential to the image, as desire exists first in God as plenitude and is the God-given capacity in humanity that ultimately leads us to God as we desire to be filled with his Spirit and presence. If God is someone we love, then desire will be an integral aspect of our relationship with Godself.

Timothy R. Gaines and Shawna Songer Gaines also develop this idea, placing the emphasis on healthy sexual desire, the sanctification of the flesh, and fanning flames of desire into worship and service.[6] In response to particularly repressive views of sex and desire, they argue that Christians need to understand more about the process of sanctifying sexual desire so as to see it more as a creative force in relation to God and one another. So they write, "In the power of the Spirit, we surrender our bodies in the likeness of Christ to be part of this sanctified creation, bringing glory to the Father."[7] Sanctification, they claim, "frees our sexual desires to be oriented toward the one who is redeeming our bodies in the consummation of all creation."[8] Per-

---

4. Coakley, *God, Sexuality, and the Self*, 1.

5. Coakley, *God, Sexuality, and the Self*, 9 (italics original).

6. Gaines and Gaines, "Uncovering Christ."

7. Gaines and Gaines, "Uncovering Christ," 105.

8. Gaines and Gaines, "Uncovering Christ," 105.

ceiving sexual desire as integral to the image raises some interesting questions especially in light of the prevalence of disordered sexual relations in the contemporary West, fueled by the tidal wave of graphic and easily accessible pornography, which has been normalized in our society. It is often noted that we live in an age of hypersexualization and that this is affecting even very young children. Thus navigating questions around eroticism will be complex, but is perhaps pressing.

In summary, despite a substantial amount of chaos and certainly conflict in thinking around identity, sex, gender, and sexuality in the West, the positive aspects of these developments are that in general, people are far more tolerant of difference than they have been in the past, and who and what people say they are, is by and large acknowledged and respected. Thus, many of these developments are to be welcomed, as they offer greater freedom of expression and freedom from oppression than Christians and all people have had in previous centuries.

As a final point on this issue though, many people proceed in the discussion on the basis that what is essentially masculine and essentially feminine in terms of character traits, behavior, attire, and the like is obvious. However, the Bible is remarkably silent on this issue. There are no gender stereotypes in the Scriptures, no descriptions of precisely what it means to be a man or a woman, or even what it means to be manly or womanly, masculine or feminine. Moreover, where we do see an example of a man devoted to God, in Jesus Christ, we see that he encompasses all the character traits and attributes that we expect in both men and women. Scripture tells us a story of men and women called to serve God on the basis of their submission to him; their ability to step out in faith; their gifts, both natural and supernatural; and their willingness to obey. The writers of the Old and New Testaments were not very concerned to tell men how to be men and women how to be women, but to tell a story about how all people can be in a relationship with God. We now turn to another contemporary question, that of disability.

DISABILITY STUDIES

There are many accounts of the imago Dei in relation to those who have disabilities of different kinds, and it is not possible to do them all justice by any means. Of significance in contemporary theology is the argument that certain disabilities should not be viewed as a lack of some type of sought-after perfection but instead should be viewed as integral to both the individual concerned and as part of physical, mental, and emotional life, and, therefore, not aberrant but normal. In other words, they are not even disabilities at all and do not need "fixing," in order for a person to become like those without those so called disabilities. This view can be seen in the work of Jane S. Deland, who argues for a "liberatory theology" of disability. According to her, we have for too long been captive to images of God "which view wholeness as physical and bodily perfection as the theological norm."[9] Against the idea that people often play off what they perceive to be the "perfect" and "normal" prelapsarian world against impairment and disease, which is then deemed to be a result of sin,[10] Deland explores how disability might give us a deeper insight not only into ourselves as images of God, but into God himself.

Thus, Deland rejects "the myth of original perfection and uniformity which has no scriptural basis," and argues

9. Deland, "Images of God through the Lens of Disability," 51.

10. Deland, "Images of God through the Lens of Disability," 51–52.

for a fundamental goodness in creation that persists beyond the fall and still pertains in creation.[11] "God saw everything that he had made, and indeed, it was very good" (Gen 1:31). In Deland's view, vulnerability, dependence, and disability are not perversions of God's creation, but "rather integral parts of its essence and infinite variety which God proclaimed 'very good.'"[12] This particular view is prevalent in disability studies—the idea that vulnerability, frailty, and interdependence are part of what is truly human and are aspects of life that enrich our lives and relationships, not detract from them.

In a previous section, on the question of women and the image, we touched on the issue of how we see ourselves in God with specific reference to Christ, and on how the imago Christi relates to the imago Dei. Given that Jesus Christ was a first-century Jewish male, is it necessary to see our own lives mirrored in Christ's earthly life? People have different answers to this question. Nancy Eiesland posits a reconceptualization of the symbol of Christ on the cross where we see a disabled and whole God at the same time, and herein lies the imago Dei.[13] As Deland points out, Eiesland's work has significant theological implications. Firstly, if God is disabled, the link between sin and disability is severed while the goal of physical perfection is rejected. Deland writes, "Physical disability must be seen as a point of connection with God rather than as a taboo to be avoided. By acknowledging the existence of both evident and 'hidden' disabilities, as portrayed by Jesus' 'pierced' side, and by accepting the image of the disabled God, Christ's body, the Church, may allow people with disabilities to participate

---

11. Deland, "Images of God through the Lens of Disability," 52.

12. Deland, "Images of God through the Lens of Disability," 52.

13. Eiesland, *The Disabled God*, 98.

fully in that body."[14] Quoting Eiesland, she writes, "Such a liberatory theology of disability would bear witness to the The fact that 'Our bodies participate in the Imago Dei, not in spite of our impairments and contingencies, but through them.'"[15]

The growth in disability studies highlights the need for much more discernment in how we view various conditions and states of being when we decide what it looks like to be physically healthy and well. In other words, not everything that looks like a disability to an able-bodied person is viewed in that way by the person who lives with that condition. In addition to this, we need to be careful not to idolize physical perfection over everything else. We have an obsession in the West with physical perfection (although what is deemed to be perfect is questionable in the first place), and a drive to full health over other goals in life. As Deland points out, "the ultimate evil that can befall humans is not disease, disability, or death, but separation from the love and grace of God."[16] In addition to this, many Pentecostal and charismatic traditions have embraced the idea that physical health and well-being is the goal of existence. As a result, those with disabilities are regularly subjected to prayer for healing when they have not sought this prayer and would not, if asked. Of course, physical health is associated with well-being in general and the healing of physical ailments is normative in the Gospels as well as in many church traditions. Thus, even if we did not believe in miraculous healing, compassion drives the church to pray for those who are visibly suffering. However, the point here is establishing in the first place whether a person perceives

14. Deland, "Images of God through the Lens of Disability," 61.

15. Deland, "Images of God through the Lens of Disability," 61, quoting Eiesland, *The Disabled God*, 101 (Deland's italics).

16. Deland, "Images of God through the Lens of Disability," 59.

the condition in which they live as something they wish to leave behind as well as hearing from those we consider "disabled" about how they perceive themselves.

As Deland goes on to note, this has implications for the significance of the Eucharist and how we understand the value of brokenness and wholeness in the world and in the church. The broken body of Christ as central to our worship affirms the broken but whole existence of those whose bodies, like his, are broken and vulnerable. This narrative militates against a concept of a perfect and flawless existence and opens up many possibilities for thinking around finding God's presence in brokenness and loss. In my view, there is a propitious turn in the development of the doctrine of the image arising out of disability studies. Here, as we have seen with Comensoli, Swinton, and others, we find a call to account for the dependence, vulnerability, and disability inherent in human lives in order for the doctrine to have anything meaningful to say to everyday existence. Moreover, although it often seems these debates are framed from the perspective of those who are permanently disabled, given the inevitability of some kind of intellectual or physical disability that most of the human population will face in their lifetime, it is important that our understanding of the imago Dei is capacious enough to accommodate all states of life.

ON HUMANS AS CREATORS

On a different note, another development within contemporary theology in relation to the imago Dei is to bring the idea of human beings as essentially creative to the fore, made in the image of God the Creator or Artificer. This is not a new idea. In the sixteenth-century, Giorgio Vasari uses the term "artificer" of himself to signify that he was taking part in the task of creating God's image through his art.[17] And others have noted the emphasis on human beings as creators with God comes to the fore in Renaissance thinking. However, as human beings are constantly creating and inventing, the idea of creativity as essential to the image of God is a rich theme and has taken on particularly new nuances in recent years.

Human beings are endlessly imaginative, creative and inventive, and this appears to be simply a natural part of who we are and not tied to any concept of spiritual gifts or even a conscious relationship with God himself. Boyan Slat, the inventor and CEO of the Ocean Cleanup method and program, a unique and successful method for ridding oceans and rivers of plastic, says this about creativity: "Human history is a long list of things that were impossible and then were done. I've been an inventor for all my life and the feeling you get when you think about something and then see that become reality, I think there's really no better feeling than that, than the act of creation."[18] Not only does Slat not feel the need to credit God for the inspiration behind his idea, but he casts himself as a creator. In many ways, one feels that is fair enough! This would be true of many extraordinarily creative people throughout history. They see it as a natural part of what it means to be human and of who they are.

In Christian thinking, however, we would say we are creative because God is creative, but that we cannot create out of nothing because only God is able to do just that. Moreover, where process theologians might see a greater scope for human beings actually to create alongside God, within the orthodox Christian tradition, there has always

17. Vasari, *Lives of the Artists*, xii.

18. Boyan Slat, creator of The Ocean Cleanup, quoted on *Ocean Action Hub* (website) in "How the Ocean Cleanup Is Solving."

been a line between the God who creates ex nihilo, whereas human beings as part of the creation are only able to create from the stuff God made in the first place. The reason for this line is to safeguard the nature of God as other than the creation and to protect humanity from the hubris that comes from perceiving themselves as having any ultimate power over creation. In classical terms then, it is essential not to confuse the human artist's and God's acts of creation. In this sense, I think many would use the term *cocreator* advisedly, but we do see this term applied widely now in theological circles albeit in slightly different ways depending on who is using the term and why. The term *cocreator* with God, then, will be used to imply varying degrees of initiative in the act of creation attributed to the individual/s, and can be utilized in multiple spheres where we see the remarkable creativity of human beings: the arts, technology, medicine, food, agriculture, philosophy, language, science, education, and so forth. The list goes on and on.

As we have touched on previously, the idea of human beings as creators with a specifically God-given role in relation to the care of creation has also come to the fore. Richter develops this in her work, describing human beings as "stewards of Eden."[19] Harking back to the creation story and the picture of the first humans as those who tended a garden, Richter argues that humanity has the responsibility of stewarding creation's resources in a way that benefits the whole of creation, the entire ecosystem, rather than just an immediate human need. Here she addresses the unbridled consumerism so rampant in the West and the need to be aware of the ethics of the supply chain in its entirety rather than being concerned just with lowering the price of the end product, regardless of the cost to the rest of the world. What we see in her work is the general trend

19. See Richter, *Stewards of Eden.*

toward a chastened and humbler view of humanity's role on the earth in relation to creation that is often expressed in contemporary theologies. Given the state the planet is in due to the rapacious greed of its human inhabitants, the language of dominion and rule now appears outdated and inappropriately hubristic to many. Thus it has given way to terms such as *stewardship*, *responsibility*, and even service. In addition to this, we see the language of cocreator applied in relation to how human beings might be able to create conditions that will benefit the rest of humanity in bringing the peace or *shalom*, beauty, and goodness of God's kingdom here on earth.

Linked to creativity, but with a different emphasis, is the ability to imagine how God might bring something into being that cannot yet be seen and perhaps has never yet been seen. This is called a prophetic imagination and is often deemed to be a godlike attribute. This prophetic imagination not only gives the ability to see the potential of what the Spirit might bring into being but is able to galvanize the church to pray and to work towards this end. This can function in relation to individuals and what they might become in Christ, to churches, organizations, and even nations. It is often understood in the context of the establishing of justice and the righting of wrongs.[20] When genuinely Spirit-inspired, it is able to raise faith and fuel hope. Ultimately, of course, Christians are called to imagine that God is both willing and able to recreate the cosmos into a new heavens and a new earth where there will be no more death, mourning, crying, or pain for the old order of things will have passed away (Rev 21:4).

20. For this see Brueggemann, *The Prophetic Imagination*.

HUMANITY AND TECHNOLOGY

In relation to the question of human beings as cocreators, one of the most interesting and probably challenging new discussions for our time surround the relationship of humanity to technology, or *transhumanism*. Stephen Garner describes the philosophy of transhumanism in the following terms: transhumanism is "a movement that asserts that human beings can now use technology to control their own evolution and destiny, becoming, to all intents and purposes, god-like."[21] Thus far, theologians have not particularly engaged with these developments in the mainstream. As Garner points out, theologians are more inclined to engage with the ethics of technologies "such as genetic manipulation, reproductive technologies, and the cloning of organisms" than they are to explore questions that arise from the huge and far-reaching developments in digital technologies. These developments include the fields of "artificial intelligence, robotics, virtual reality, nanotechnology, genetic engineering and longevity research," which Garner notes are now talked about regularly in a range of popular media and are affecting the shape of public policy. Garner's research centers on the narratives of apprehension and hope surrounding technological and digital developments in relation to the imago Dei.[22] He uses the metaphor of God as a hacker. Technologists speak of "the Hack," in the context of the search for transcendence. "Often likened to the Holy Grail, it is that one act or work of novelty and creativity that transcends all others, and will bring the hacker completion."[23] Here Garner cites the act of the incarnation as the quintessential example of the Hack—an act that is

21. Garner, "Transhumanism and the imago Dei," 2.

22. Garner, "Transhumanism and the imago Dei," 3.

23. Garner, "Transhumanism and the imago Dei," 219.

wholly creative, novel, and surprising. In his view, when human beings perform these kind of feats, they image God. With the rapid pace of scientific and technological development that we face today, it is no wonder there are people who believe they can "play God" in this sense.

For this reason, and as Garner points out, technological advances and the modification of human life, bodies, minds, and even genes through science have long been the source of apprehension and the subject of popular imagination. From as far back as Mary Shelley's *Frankenstein* (1818), one novel or film after another has expressed a deep-seated fear of what might happen to human beings if we modify too much of what we are, or if we create other beings that then have power over us. This fiction explores the terrible things that might happen if human beings usurp their creator and begin to play God. On the other hand, a sober assessment of how scientific and technological advances have vastly improved our quality of life across the globe in the last century demonstrates so many of the advantages of these discoveries and inventions. For all the fears around artificial intelligence, robots in one form or another will be a normal part of life in the future.

A multitude of ethical questions surrounds developments in science and technology and the unprecedented ability that men and women now possess that allows them to modify life for good or ill. We cannot discuss them all here, but many of them relate to how we understand human beings as made in the image of God. Clearly, what it means to be human no longer looks like it did in previous centuries. Now we face questions around enhancement, implants, sophisticated prosthetics, hybridity, and genetic modification. It is no longer a given that human beings need to live with what they have been given. A human being is now editable in multiple ways. From a Christian perspective, and as Garner argues, there will be a need for the gifts of wisdom and charity as we advance into these new worlds. How do we use these tools to build a better world, and what does that look like? The need for theological engagement is clear.

There is a further, related but slightly different question that is also under discussion, and that is how human beings relate to the robotic world and the creation of artificial intelligence with which we interact. Is there any sense in which the things we create, derived from how we think and function, can be said to be made in the image of God and if so, how? Needless to say, we can only answer these questions from a foundation of robust theological engagement on the questions of what it means to be and to become the image of God.[24]

THE EIKON AND THE SPIRITUAL BATTLE

Contemporary studies on the image of God are diverse, rich, challenging, and rapidly evolving. There is no one answer or perspective that gives us the full picture, and so, finally, to demonstrate the variety within the discussion, I highlight the work of Gabrielle Thomas on Gregory of Nazianzus as an example of retrieving ancient perspectives for a modern worldview. Thomas mines Gregory's thought for an account of the imago Dei that, she argues, encompasses the functional, ontological, and relational and also proves to be christological, pneumatological, and inclusive of all persons.[25] As we noted in Chapter 1, it is a misrepresentation to state that all early church thinkers saw the image as a disembodied soul, and here Thomas makes the point that

24. See Herzfeld. "Creating in Our Own Image."

25. See Thomas, *The Image of God*; Thomas, "Vulnerable, Yet Divine,"; Thomas, "The Human Icon."

Gregory sees the image in the whole person, the unity of body, soul, and spirit. Throughout her work on the imago Dei, Thomas refers to the image in the Greek, *eikon*, and in the feminine, "she/her," respecting the feminine grammatical gender of the Greek noun, and thus opening new avenues for thinking about the image itself simply through the language chosen. She also prefers the term *eikon* over "image" in order to convey the sense of the visibility of the human.[26] Thomas traces Gregory's view of the image in relation to *theosis*, highlighting his understanding of the *eikon* as divine, yet vulnerable. Being made in the image of God means being created for union with the divine creator and thus divinized. Being made flesh and blood, however, makes the *eikon* vulnerable to the destruction that can come through the world, the flesh, and the devil. In Gregory's view the enemy of humanity, Lucifer, is consumed with envy and consequently, is constantly seeking to destroy the *eikon*. Thus, human existence is characterized by a battle with the spiritual forces arraigned against humanity. As Thomas notes, "Drawing his inspiration from biblical and extra-biblical narratives, Gregory locates the human *eikon* in a cosmological battle with the forces of evil."[27] In this context, the *eikon* is transformed through baptism and the power of the Holy Spirit into godlikeness, but not without a struggle. Thomas writes:

> The Spirit's involvement in the *theosis* of the *eikon* means that the *eikon* moves towards being enlightened, and thus gaining life and increasing in her likeness to God. This evokes the envy of the devil, who steps in and attempts to lead the *eikon* into darkness and sin. The devil does not want the *eikon* to fulfill her destiny in becoming

26. Thomas, "The Human Icon," 170.
27. Thomas, *The Image of God*, 118.

a god, which means that any enlightenment and enlivening causes him great vexation. However, the *eikon* is not left without help and protection when the enemy is waging war on her: 'Don't be afraid of the battle. Protect yourself with water, protect yourself with the Spirit, in whom every single burning missile of the Enemy is put out.'[28]

Thomas argues that Gregory sees the human being as "porous" to the spiritual realm—both to God and the devil. She quite rightly points out that the devil receives very little attention in theological scholarship but is, however, "central to Gregory's approach to the existence of the *eikon*."[29] In her view, the lack of theological attention the devil receives results from the effects of the eighteenth-century Enlightenment on Western culture. Thanks to the Enlightenment we see modernity's "scepticism towards transcendent beings such as angels and demons."[30] As she notes, however, when early Christian scholars pay due attention to the devil, it is often to the devil as the enemy of the *eikon*.[31] It is important to note that despite the Western dismissal of these aspects of the spiritual life, an understanding of the reality and activity of angels, demons, and spirits is normative in the Majority World. In addition to this, with the growth of Pentecostal and charismatic churches, theologians will need to familiarize themselves with how these realities are understood by a vast number of Christians throughout the world in relation to the work of God in the world and in a human being.

28. Taken from Gregory of Nazianzus, quoted in Thomas, *The Image of God*, 133.

29. Thomas, *The Image of God*, 30.

30. Thomas, *The Image of God*, 30.

31. Thomas, *The Image of God*, 32.

Thomas's work not only resonates with a Pentecostal and charismatic worldview but is, of course, consistent with Eastern Orthodoxy, rooted as it is in Gregory's thought. As we see above, human beings are not alone in the battle, having the protection of the water of baptism and the Spirit, who functions as a shield in the battle. The Spirit is at work transforming the human being into the divine image—*theosis*. The *eikon* increases in divinity quantitatively and not qualitatively, because only God is divine; but human beings may increase in godlikeness. Thomas highlights Gregory's vision of the human *eikon* as dynamic, alive, and mysterious. "By this, I mean that the *eikon* does not represent a static quality within the human person, but is a living and breathing *eikon*, created with the potential to become like God, or, in Gregory's words, 'divine.'" This process, however, remains a mystery.[32]

I have continued to make the point that I cannot possibly cover or even touch on every topic in contemporary theology of the image of God. My hope in these last two chapters has been to provide a picture of some of the breadth and diversity of perspectives in contemporary scholarship while bearing in mind that this is really only a snapshot of the range of views out there. What is abundantly clear is the discussion is open for much debate and can be taken in a multitude of directions. No doubt this is precisely what will happen in years to come.

DISCUSSION QUESTIONS

1. Have you been influenced primarily by a traditional or a progressive view of sex, gender, and sexuality?

32. Thomas, *The Image of God*, 18.

2. What do you think about the history of celibacy in the church?

3. Do you think of desire as essentially a negative or a positive aspect of human life?

4. What teaching on the image of God and disability have you received?

5. Does something have to be fully human to image God?

6. Does the language of spiritual warfare make any sense to you?

CONCLUSION

INTRODUCTION

As we have now seen, it is abundantly clear that there is no single, closed definition of the imago Dei to which all might assent. Even if we have a preference for one specific perspective, it is unlikely that one definition will succeed in saying all we might want to say about how humanity images God or where that image lies. The doctrine of the imago Dei is multifaceted and constantly evolving. It corresponds both to what we believe to be true of God and to what we believe to be true of humanity; thus each generation and each culture will develop and revise this doctrine, bringing new insights and perspectives to what this claim means for humanity, for God, and for our relations with one another and the world. To my mind, the open-endedness of the conversation is a strength rather than a weakness. It contributes to the sense of mystery associated with this doctrine and reminds us of the need for an element of apophaticism in regard to what we can and cannot articulate. In conclusion, I will highlight some doctrinal foundations to a Christian understanding of the imago Dei while also drawing together some final observations with respect to theological and anthropological perspectives for continued reflection.

THE IMAGO DEI, THE IMAGO CHRISTI, AND THE GIFT OF THE SPIRIT

The first issue to note is that a Christian theology of the imago Dei will entail both a universal and a particular expression rooted as it is in the creation stories in Genesis (which apply to all humanity) and shaped by the person of Christ—the image of the invisible God, the firstborn over all creation. In a sense the imago Christi modifies and gives definition to the imago Dei and vice versa, in that when the Son comes to earth, he comes as a human being just like us. We interpret one through the lens of the other. As we have seen, interpreting the imago Dei via the imago Christi has traditionally given rise to a two-tier perspective of the imago Dei: those who are made in God's image by virtue of being created by God viz. all humanity, and those who are deemed to be in Christ, who are being re-formed into God's image and likeness through union with Christ and the indwelling of the Holy Spirit. There is also a clear progression to traditional image theology in that those who are in Christ are being transformed from one degree of glory to another over time until they are fully transformed into the image and likeness of God in the presence of God as they behold him face-to-face in the beatific vision. As I noted in the beginning, this two-tiered conception of the imago Dei is applied very differently depending on how one views the efficacy of the atonement. It is not possible to outline all the different positions in relation to questions of who might be saved and who might not and why, but broadly speaking, a universalist would posit that all humanity will eventually be saved and thus be in Christ anyway whereas those who hold to a limited atonement would separate humanity into those who have made a confession of faith in Christ and thus are saved and those who have not and so are not. In other words, defining the imago Dei through the imago Christi is not necessarily an exclusivist claim, but it might be, depending on who is making that claim.

It is important when discussing the imago Christi not to neglect the pneumatological aspect of the image. An early account of this can be found in Cyril of Alexandria (376–444 CE). Cyril has a robust and well-developed pneumatology in relation to the imago Dei, tracing the impress of the imago Dei back to the Spirit. Cyril writes, "And God created man, in the Image of God created He him. But that through the Spirit he was sealed unto the Divine Image, himself again taught us, saying, And breathed into his nostrils the breath of life. For the Spirit at once began both to put life into His formation and in a Divine manner to impress His own Image thereon."[1] Cyril posits that as humanity sank deeper into sin, the Spirit's impress become fainter until the Spirit departs altogether. God, however, has pity on his flock and in his goodness, hastens to save them. He decrees "to trans-element human nature anew to the pristine Image through the Spirit."[2]

According to Cyril, humanity is raised up in dignity in the Son and by the power of the Holy Spirit. This is a restoration of the first dignity accorded to humanity by the gift of God's breath of life through which "man" becomes a living soul. The bestowing of the image in the first place comes through the Spirit, as does the restoration of the image after the fall. Cyril views the receiving of the Spirit by Jesus Christ at his baptism as the beginning of the gift of the Spirit given to humanity. It is not that Christ needs the Spirit in any way, as it is his Spirit, which he also gives, but as the sinless but nevertheless fully human image, he receives the Spirit so that we too might receive the restoring

1. Cyril of Alexandria, *Commentary on John*, 1:32–33.
2. Cyril of Alexandria, *Commentary on John*, 1:32–33.

Spirit in him.[3] The Spirit is the one who restores human nature to wholeness. "For the Spirit reforms into incorruption that which was by sin corrupted, and fashions into newness of life that which was obsolete through apathy, and verging to decay."[4] We will come back to the traditional perspective on the imago Dei, but first we recap briefly how recent developments in Western theology have challenged certain traditional perspectives.

RECENT DEVELOPMENTS

As we have seen, recent developments in Western theology are often shaped by postmodern sensibilities around exclusion in any form, and this has had a significant impact on image theology. These sensibilities, naturally, tend to drive theological reflection in a more universal direction in order to ensure that all are included, whatever their relation to God, their state of mind, their state of being, and so forth. This emphasis on inclusion is welcomed by some and not by others. This depends upon prior theological commitments in that those of a more conservative bent draw more definite lines between those whom they perceive to be incorporated into the body of Christ, the church, and those who are outside the body of Christ, the church. Others, however, reject any narrative of exclusion and formulate their theology accordingly, to claim that in some way all are or will be included in the end. There is also, as we have seen, some resistance in contemporary thought to a definition of the imago Dei that is teleological, promissory, or deferred.

This is also clearly a reaction against the traditional two-tiered and progression-based views of the image, which all have a sense of the teleological, promissory, and

3. Cyril of Alexandria, *Commentary on John*, 1:32–33.
4. Cyril of Alexandria, *Commentary on John*, 17:18–19.

deferred about them, predicated as they are on what is to come in the eschaton. In addition, in pursuit of a more expansive definition of the imago Dei, scholars have sought to enumerate theologies of the image that amalgamate the ontological, functional, and relational views rather than opting just for one perspective. Further, we have noted that there is a renewed emphasis on the image of God as a verb rather than a noun, with a strong justice element to the idea of what it means "to image" God. And we have also seen that biblical scholars bring a strong theology of the image rooted in the Genesis texts. These functional perspectives have had an impact on contemporary theologies of creation care and have raised other ethical issues around the witness of the church in the world, along with questions around what it means to participate in the kingdom of God in the here and now. All these moves have made for a richer conversation around the question of what it means to be made in the image of God.

It is understandable that many reject the idea that those who are not Christians are somehow a lesser version of the image and likeness of God than those who are. This can appear to be a harsh and exclusivist perspective. Not only this, but it is not as though the church has distinguished itself through the ages as an exemplary sign of God's presence here on earth. There have been times when the church excels in loving God and loving others, seeking and enacting justice, and walking humbly with God and others. There are also times, however, when the church's actions are abominable, and Christians' treatment of others outrightly wicked. Given this, it is no wonder that there is resistance to the idea that Christians reflect the image of God to the world in a special way so that many prefer to appeal to the general sense of the whole of humanity made in God's image in order to communicate both the innate dignity and worth of all human beings and the complete and utter equality of all human beings regardless of their faith, culture, skin color, sex, or other traits. However, to conclude this little book, and with those sensitivities in mind, I wish to return briefly to the traditional view of humanity remade into the image and likeness of God in Christ, as this narrative also has much to offer by way of redemption and healing. For as much as I appreciate the offense of a theology that appears to separate the Christian from the non-Christian in image theology, there are also aspects to the restoration of the image in Christ that are deeply redemptive, which I would be loath to ignore.

THE RESTORATION OF THE IMAGE IN CHRIST

The Judaeo-Christian story begins with the story of the creation and subsequent fall of humanity through wilful disobedience or tragic immaturity or perhaps both. Whether we attribute this to immaturity, to pride or to outright rebellion, the results of the story are the same. Human beings are expelled from the garden and are not able to dwell in the presence of God in the same way they had done before. It is a story, not strictly of separation as some imagine, but of alienation. God and humanity are alienated through the refusal of human beings to live as God purposed for them to live—in peace and harmony with himself, one another, and creation. Instead, they spiral in the opposite direction, and so the story accounts for the destructive capacity of human beings that leads to the horrors perpetrated by one human being against another. The immaturity, pride, and wickedness of humanity goes down from one generation to another as it becomes clear that being born into a fallen world means being born a fallen creature with the incapability of saving oneself from sin. This is the warning that God gives to Cain as he contemplates the murder of his brother—that if he does not master sin, sin will master him (Gen 4:6–7).

The story tells us that sin and evil, as it were, roots itself in the human heart and cannot be uprooted by sheer will. And so the apostle Paul writes, "All have sinned and fall short of the glory of God'" (Rom 3:23). As Paul describes in Rom 3, this theology of the inescapable nature and the universality of sin also has its own uncompromisingly egalitarian foundation, as no one is able to rise above the status of sinful humanity of their own accord. All human beings are sinners in need of salvation and are thus all equal beneficiaries of the grace and forgiveness of God . No one may claim a superior status over anyone else. As Paul also writes, "May I never boast of anything except the cross of our Lord Jesus Christ, by which the world has been crucified to me, and I to the world" (Gal 6:14). The idea of the restoration of the image of God in those who are united to Christ, therefore, is predicated solely on the recognition of the idea that these are the people who have recognized their sinful state and have received the grace of God extended to humanity through the cross of Christ. It is not really a story primarily of the worth of those who are now in Christ, but a story of the worth of the whole of humanity, more specifically, the worth of sinners to God.

Unfortunately, however, many denominations over the years have somehow seemed to communicate the worthlessness of the sinner to God, his wrath toward them, and his negative judgment of them, especially once they have become one of the saved! I believe many people outside the church have the impression that they are by nature objects of wrath rather than by nature objects of love, which often, tragically, only alienates them further from God. In the Eastern Orthodox tradition, the "natural" state of humanity is a person created and moulded by God. Sin is a distortion of the natural state and affects the way a person behaves and responds to others and the world, but sin cannot destroy the nature created by God in his image, because nothing created is able to have that much power over God. Andrew Louth, in discussing the thought of Maximus the Confessor, writes this, "The fact that the Fall does not touch the level of nature does not entail that the effects of the Fall are superficial, simply that no creature has the power to overthrow the fundamental design of the Creator. But the Fall does mean that fallen creatures exist in a world they can no longer understand."[5] This perspective speaks not only of the inherent value of the human, but also of the overarching purposes of God towards humanity, to save human beings because he loves them.

Something of this Eastern perspective captures the worth of humanity to God, but whatever we believe to be the case in relation to the image—whether it remains intact in some way, whether it is tainted, broken, or lost altogether—what we do know is that Jesus came to seek and save that which was lost out of love for the world. God only comes, in Christ, to save sinners because God *loves* sinners (Luke 19:10). Athanasius, insightfully, makes the link between creation, image theology, and salvation, explaining that it would be unthinkable for God to abandon what he made in the first place. Instead, it is entirely fitting that God should come himself, in the perfect image of humanity to save and remake the image that belongs to him through drawing humanity back to himself in Christ. Thus, Jesus Christ manifests the love of God in a unique and salvific way through his sacrifice in the incarnation, his suffering and death in the crucifixion, and his resurrection. Moreover, the gift of the Spirit, poured out on all flesh at Pentecost and to the present day is primarily the unbounded

5. Louth, *Maximus the Confessor*, 56.

and indiscriminate gift of God's love poured into the hearts of humanity. The Spirit re-forms and remolds humanity precisely by persuading human beings that they are indeed loved beyond measure by God and that they please him.

At Christ's baptism, the Spirit descends, and the voice of the Father is heard over the Son, "This is my beloved Son in whom I am well pleased." As the same Spirit falls on humanity, so the voice of God the creator is spoken over individuals, assuring them of the love of the Father for his children. Paul speaks of the Spirit as the one through whom the love of God is poured into our hearts, delivering us from slavery to fear so that we, too, with Jesus Christ, might be able to cry out to God as our own Father. The Spirit witnesses to us, or convinces us, that we too are beloved children of God (Rom 5:5; 8:14–17). As Henri Nouwen writes, "all I want to say to you is, You are the Beloved, and all I hope is that you can hear these words as spoken to you with all the tenderness and force that love can hold. My only desire is to make these words reverberate in every corner of your being—You are the Beloved."[6] Image-of-God theology seen through the lens of the imago Christi and the pouring out of the Spirit is not a story of exclusion but of inclusion, and an inclusion that leads to restoration and freedom from the distortion of sin, brokenness, enmity, division, alienation, and isolation.

The posture of the church, therefore, can never be one of superiority over the world, but only one of humility and welcome towards the world, for this is what we see in the incarnation. In Chapter 3, we saw McCormack and Craig Blomberg arguing for the moral-relational view of the image. This is the idea that the image of God manifests in the holiness of God's people through holy living. This is not something that we achieve, however, lest we boast about

6. Nouwen, *Life of the Beloved*, 29.

our achievements, but only something that God brings about in his people, and only something that is sustained through his continuing, loving presence. Jürgen Moltmann writes, "The church is holy because it is sanctified through Christ's activity in and on it . . . Holiness consists of being made holy, in sanctification, the subject of the activity being God (I Thess. 5.23; II Thess. 2.13)." He goes on,

> God sanctifies his church by calling the godless through Christ, by justifying sinners, and by accepting the lost. The communion or community of the saints—or the holy or sanctified—is therefore always at the same time the community of sinners; and the sanctified church is always at the same time the sinful church. Through its continual prayer 'forgive us our trespasses,' it recognizes itself as being in sin and at the same time as being holy in the divine forgiveness of sins . . . It is in this very thing that its sanctification, and consequently its holiness, consists.[7]

THE VALUE OF IMAGE THEOLOGY

Image of God theology, therefore, is really a great leveling doctrine. Thus there is enormous potential in image theology, through the recognition of all humanity as made in God's image, for what Willie James Jennings calls "redemptive theology," i.e., theologies that can bring healing and reconciliation, and justice where there is brokenness, enmity, and oppression. One of the positive developments of the last few decades is the work that has been done on the effects of abuse and trauma on individuals, families, and communities and just how destructive this can be. Knowing more of the destructive and deeply damaging effects of

7. Moltmann, *The Church*, 353.

abusive actions and words and how they erode a person's sense of value, worth, and dignity means that we have a better insight into what might need to be done to counteract these actions and words and the long-term effects of the same. What we see in image theology is great potential to bring out how it speaks to the inherent value and worth of a human life and hence its restorative and redemptive value.

Understanding the imago Dei in the broad sense from Gen 1 communicates a wealth of ideas, all of which highlight the inherent worth of humanity to God. To have been created intentionally, imagined in the mind of God, and then brought into being communicates something profound about a person's intrinsic worth. It speaks—you are loved; you are wanted; you are valued. Further to this, to have been created as some kind of reflection or embodiment of the divine serves only to strengthen the idea that human beings are of infinite worth and beauty. As Deland points out, human beings were created "very good." It is not possible to have been created in the image and likeness of God without having been created good. The redemptive aspect of the Christian story is firstly that despite being lost and broken, there is yet great value, placed on a human life by God. Secondly, we see that what is lost and broken can be found and remade, refashioned into a thing of beauty. With Christ, there is the possibility of forgiveness of both ourselves and our enemies, and this is the hope of rebirth, and with this rebirth, an elevation to becoming a coheir with Christ. Cyril of Alexandria writes, "For we are adopted, mounting up to excellency above nature through the will of Him that honoured us, and gaining the title of gods and sons because of Christ that dwelleth in us through the Holy Ghost."[8]

8. Cyril of Alexandria, *Commentary on John*, 5.18.

So while I remain sensitive to the idea that we do not want to communicate too much that is promissory or deferred if it might detract from a person's worth here and now, I would not want to lose the idea that we have a promise and hope of a better world. This is not to say that we remain passive and accepting of the status quo of this world while we just wait for the better world that is coming—the new heavens and the new earth. The functional aspects of image-of-God theology cast a completely different light on how Christians are called to respond to creation in the here and now. Those who bear God's image or name represent him here on earth, which entails treating others and the creation in accordance with the value that God places on the same.

Finally, I wish to highlight the theme of glory associated with image theology in the idea of human beings as bearers of God's glory. Karl Barth writes that glory (*doxa*) in the New Testament "means not only the honour which God Himself has or prepares for Himself, but also that which the creature gives Him, as well as finally the honour which He for His part gives to the creature."[9] To glorify, then, means "both to honour, praise, extol and glorify as a creaturely action and also to transfigure as a divine." Thus, to be glorified has a twofold meaning of "both the glorification of God by the creature and of the creature by God."[10] Barth goes on to make the point that the service of God by humanity "means that the creature is taken up into the sphere of divine lordship."[11] This is because his glory consists in self-giving, at the center of which is Jesus Christ. Through him, we share in God's glory.

9. Barth, *Church Dogmatics*, II/1, 670.

10. Barth, *Church Dogmatics*, II/1, 670.

11. Barth, *Church Dogmatics*, II/1, 670.

This theme is reiterated in C. S. Lewis's brief essay "The Weight of Glory."[12] Human beings are those who are created to echo gratitude back to God, to magnify and glorify him; and in doing so, they are themselves glorified and even honored. In this essay, Lewis brings out the obligation that one has to another because they too bear God's image and therefore his glory. Lewis writes this: "The load or weight or burden of my neighbour's glory should be laid daily on my back, a load so heavy that only humility can carry it, and the backs of the proud will be broken. It is a serious thing to live in a society of possible gods and goddesses, to remember that the dullest and most un-interesting person you can talk to may one day be a creature which, if you saw it now, you would be strongly tempted to worship."[13] This realization, he argues, should inform our interactions with everyone we meet: "it is immortals whom we joke with, work with, marry, snub, and exploit—immortal horrors or everlasting splendours . . . Next to the Blessed Sacrament itself, your neighbour is the holiest object presented to your senses."[14]

CONCLUSION

It is not possible to conclude the conversation of what it means for humanity to be made in the image of God, nor can we cease exploring. This should not surprise us. The doctrine of the imago Dei is multifaceted, multilayered, rich, and constantly evolving. There are multiple points of departure for thinking through what it means to be made in the image of God. We can begin with humanity itself, or with the Triune God, with Christ, or even with the Spirit. Whichever we choose, it will lead us to an abundance of

12. Lewis, "The Weight of Glory."
13. Lewis, "The Weight of Glory," 109.
14. Lewis, "The Weight of Glory," 109–10.

metaphors, concepts, and ideas with which to attempt to articulate what we mean by our claim. Further to this, it will then lead us to reflect on ethics, mission, discipleship, ecclesiology and a whole host of theological and practical concerns in relation to the doctrine. So we know that it is a doctrine we must approach humbly: humbly because it confronts us with the truth that we cannot understand everything about this claim; neither have we understood how to live it out. As I have researched this doctrine with truly vast implications to write just a very short book, I have been struck deeply by the mystery of it all. But I also see the potential for this doctrine to yield rich insights into the value, beauty, and diversity of human beings as equally precious in God's sight.

DISCUSSION QUESTIONS

1. In what ways might the Holy Spirit "form" the image of God in humanity?

2. What pastoral implications do you see in relation to the doctrine of the imago Dei?

3. In what ways to you think differently about this doctrine having read this book?

4. Do you want to make any changes as a result?

BIBLIOGRAPHY

Athanasius. *On the Incarnation of the Word.* Translated and edited by a Religious of C.S.Ms.V. Rev. ed. Crestwood, NY: St. Vladimir's Seminary Press, 1993.

Augustine. *De Trinitate.* Introduction, translation and notes by Edmund Hill, OP. Edited by John E. Rotelle, OSA. The Works of Saint Augustine 5. Hyde Park, NY: New City, 1991.

———. *On Genesis.* Introduction, translation, and notes by Edmund Hill, OP. Edited by John E. Rotelle, OSA. The Works of Saint Augustine 13. Hyde Park, NY: New City, 1999.

Barth, Karl, *Church Dogmatics.* Edited by G. W. Bromiley and T. F. Torrance. Translated by G. T. Thomson and Harold Knight. 13 vols. 1956. Reprint, Peabody, MA: Hendrickson, 2010.

Baptist, Edward E. *The Half Has Never Been Told: Slavery and the Making of American Capitalism.* New York: Basic Books, 2014.

Bauckham, Richard. *Bible and Ecology: Rediscovering the Community of Creation.* Sarum Theological Lectures. London: Darton, Longman & Todd, 2016.

Beckerleg, Catherine Leigh. "The 'Image of God' in Eden: The Creation of Mankind in Genesis 2:5—3:24 in Light of the *mīs pî pīt pî* and *wpt-r* Rituals of Mesopotamia and Ancient Egypt." PhD diss., Harvard University, 2009.

Blomberg, Craig L. "True Righteousness and Holiness: The Image of God in the New Testament." In *The Image of God in an Image Driven Age: Explorations in Theological Anthropology,* edited by Beth Felker Jones and Jeffrey W. Barbeau, 66–87. Wheaton Theology Conference Series. Downers Grove, IL: IVP Academic, 2016.

Bibliography

Briggs, Sheila. "What Is Feminist Theology?" In *The Oxford Handbook of Feminist Theology*, edited by Mary McClintock Fulkerton and Sheila Briggs, 73–106. Oxford Handbooks in Religion and Theology. Oxford: Oxford University Press, 2012.

Brock, Brian, and John Swinton, eds. *Disability in the Christian Tradition: A Reader*. Grand Rapids: Eerdmans, 2012.

Brueggemann, Walter. *The Prophetic Imagination*. 40th ann. ed. Minneapolis: Fortress, 2018.

Brunner, Emil, and Karl Barth. *Natural Theology: Comprising "Nature and Grace" by Professor Dr. Emil Brunner and the Reply "No!" by Dr Karl Barth*. 1946. Reprint, Eugene, OR: Wipf & Stock, 2002.

Calvin, John. *Institutes of the Christian Religion*. Translated by Henry Beveridge. 1845. Reprint, Peabody, MA: Hendrickson, 2008.

Coakley, Sarah. *God, Sexuality, and the Self: An Essay 'On the Trinity'*. Cambridge: Cambridge University Press, 2013.

Comensoli, Peter A. *In God's Image: Recognizing the Profoundly Impaired as Persons*. Eugene, OR. Cascade Books, 2018.

Cortez, Marc. "The Madness in Our Method: Christology as the Necessary Starting Point for Theological Anthropology." In *The Ashgate Research Companion to Theological Anthropology*, edited by Joshua R. Farris and Charles Taliaferro, 15–26. An Ashgate Research Companion. Farnham, Surrey, UK: Ashgate, 2015.

Crisp, Oliver D. "A Christological Model of the Imago Dei." In *The Ashgate Research Companion to Theological Anthropology*, edited by Joshua R. Farris and Charles Taliaferro, 217–29. An Ashgate Research Companion. Farnham, Surrey, UK: Ashgate, 2015.

Cunningham, Conor. "Why Study Nature and Grace? with Dr. Conor Cunningham." https://www.youtube.com/watch?v=C8jbytgfMjU/.

Cyril of Alexandria. *Commentary on John*. Translated by P. E. Pusey. Riverside, CA: Ephesians Four Group, 2018. Kindle ed.

Daly, Mary. *Beyond God the Father: Toward a Philosophy of Women's Liberation*. Boston: Beacon, 1985.

DeFranza, Megan. "Journeying from the Bible to Christian Ethics in Search of Common Ground." In *Two Views on Homosexuality, the Bible, and the Church*, edited by William Loader et al., 69–101. Counterpoints: Bible and Theology. Grand Rapids: Zondervan, 2016.

Deland, Jane S. "Images of God through the Lens of Disability." *Journal of Religion, Disability and Health* 3/2 (1999) 47–81.

Eiesland, Nancy L. *The Disabled God: Toward a Liberatory Theology of Disability*. Nashville: Abingdon, 1994.

Bibliography

Gaines, Timothy R., and Shawna Songer Gaines. "Uncovering Christ: Sexuality in the Image of the Invisible God." In *The Image of God in an Image Driven Age: Explorations in Theological Anthropology*, edited by Beth Felker Jones and Jeffrey W. Barbeau, 91–106. Wheaton Theology Conference Series. Downers Grove, IL: IVP Academic, 2016.

Garner, Stephen Robert. "Transhumanism and the imago Dei: Narratives of Apprehension and Hope." PhD diss., University of Auckland, 2006.

Gregory of Nyssa. *On the Making of Man.* Edited by Philip Schaff. Nicene and Post-Nicene Fathers 2nd ser, 5. Buffalo: Christian Literature, 1893. Revised and edited for New Advent by Kevin Knight. http://www.newadvent.org/fathers/2914.htm/.

Grudem, Wayne. *Systematic Theology: An Introduction to Biblical Doctrine.* Grand Rapids: Zondervan, 1994.

Gunton, Colin. "The Church on Earth: The Roots of Community." In *On Being the Church: Essays on the Christian Community*, edited by Colin E. Gunton and Daniel W. Hardy, 48–80. Edinburgh: T. & T. Clark, 1989.

———. *The One, the Three and the Many: God, Creation, and the Culture of Modernity.* The Bampton Lectures 1992. Cambridge: Cambridge University Press, 2002.

———. *The Promise of Trinitarian Theology.* Edinburgh: T. & T. Clark, 1991.

Hedley, Manfred P. *The Colossian Image: Paul's Vision for Renewed Humanity and Life in Christ in Colossians.* Ashill, Norfolk, UK: Alderway, 2016.

Herzfeld, Noreen L. "Creating in Our Own Image: Artificial Intelligence and the Image of God." *Zygon* 37 (2002) 303–16.

Holmes, Stephen R. *The Holy Trinity: Understanding God's Life.* Christian Doctrines in Historical Perspective. Milton Keynes, UK: Paternoster, 2012.

Horowitz, Maryanne Cline. "The Image of God in Man: Is Woman Included?" *Harvard Theological Review* 72 (1979) 175–206.

Imes, Carmen Joy. *Bearing God's Name: Why Sinai Still Matters.* Downers Grove, IL: IVP Academic, 2019.

Irenaeus. *Against the Heresies.* Translated by Alexander Roberts and William Rambaut. Edited by Alexander Roberts et al. Ante-Nicene Fathers 1. Buffalo: Christian Literature, 1885. Revised and edited for New Advent by Kevin Knight. http://www.newadvent.org/fathers/0103.htm/.

Bibliography

Jennings, Willie James. *The Christian Imagination: Theology and the Origins of Race.* New Haven: Yale University Press, 2010.

Kilby, Karen. "Perichoresis and Projection: Problems with the Social Doctrines of the Trinity." *New Blackfriars* 81 (2000) 432–45.

Lakey, Michael J. *Image and Glory of God: 1 Corinthians 11:2–16 as a Case Study in Bible, Gender and Hermeneutics.* T. & T. Clark Library of Biblical Studies. Library of New Testament Studies 418. London: T. & T. Clark, 2010.

Lewis, C. S. "The Weight of Glory." In *Screwtape Proposes a Toast: and Other Pieces*, 94–110. Fount Paperbacks. Glasgow: Collins, 1985.

Louth, Andrew. *Maximus the Confessor.* Early Church Fathers. London: Routledge, 1996. https://azbyka.ru/otechnik/world/maximus-the-confessor-early-church-fathers/#0_123.

McConville, J. Gordon. *Being Human in God's World: An Old Testament Theology of Humanity.* Grand Rapids: Baker Acaâdemic, 2016.

McCormack, Bruce L. "Panel Discussion at Los Angeles Theology Conference." LA Theology Conference, 2015. Originally recorded here: http://latheology.com/past-years/2015locating-atonement/2015videos/. Transposed here: https://postbarthian.com/2015/02/24/bruce-mccormack-misuse-imago-dei-image-god/.

McDowell, Catherine L. "In the Image of God He Created Them: How Genesis 1:26–27 Defines the Divine–Human Relationship and Why It Matters." In *The Image of God in an Image Driven Age: Explorations in Theological Anthropology*, edited by Beth Felker Jones and Jeffrey W. Barbeau, 29–46. Wheaton Theology Conference Series. Downers Grove, IL: IVP Academic, 2016.

———. *The Image of God in the Garden of Eden: The Creation of Humankind in Genesis 2:5—3:24 in Light of the* mis pi, pit pi, *and* wpt-r *Rituals of Mesopotamia.* Siphrut 15. Winona Lake, IN: Eisenbrauns, 2015.

McFadyen, Alistair I. "Imaging God: A Theological Answer to the Anthropological Question?" *Zygon* 47 (2012) 918–33.

———. "Redeeming the Image." *International Journal for the Study of the Christian Church* 16 (2016) 108–25.

———. "The Trinity and Human Individuality: The Conditions for Relevance." *Theology* 95/10 (1992) 10–18.

Middleton, J Richard. *The Liberating Image: The Imago Dei in Genesis 1.* Grand Rapids: Brazos, 2005.

Moltmann, Jürgen, *The Church in the Power of the Spirit: A Contribution to Messianic Ecclesiology.* Translated by Margaret Kohl. London: SCM, 1977.

Bibliography

Nouwen, Henri J. M. *Life of the Beloved: Spiritual Living in a Secular World*. London: Hodder & Stoughton, 2016. Kindle ed.

Ocean Action Hub (website). "How The Ocean Cleanup Is Solving One of the Biggest Ecodisasters of Our Time." https://www.oceanactionhub.org/how-ocean-cleanup-solving-one-biggest-eco-disasters-our-time/.

Owen, John. *The Works of John Owen*. Edited by William H. Goold. 16 vols. Carlisle, PA: Banner of Truth Trust, 1965.

Peppiatt, Lucy. "Man as the Image and Glory of God and Woman as the Glory of Man: Perspicuity or Ambiguity?" *Priscilla Papers* 33/3 (2019) 12–18.

———. *Women and Worship at Corinth: Paul's Rhetorical Arguments in 1 Corinthians*. Eugene, OR: Cascade Books, 2015.

Rah, Soong Chan. "The Sin of Racism: Racialization of the Image of God." In *The Image of God in an Image Driven Age: Explorations in Theological Anthropology*, edited by Beth Felker Jones and Jeffrey W. Barbeau, 205–24. Wheaton Theology Conference Series. Downers Grove, IL: IVP Academic, 2016.

Reinders, Hans S. *Receiving the Gift of Friendship: Profound Disability, Theological Anthropology, and Ethics*. Grand Rapids: Eerdmans, 2008.

Richter, Sandra L. "A Biblical Theology of Creation Care." *Asbury Journal* 62 (2007) 67–76.

———. *Stewards of Eden: What Scripture Says about the Environment and Why It Matters*. Downers Grove, IL: IVP Academic, 2020.

Russell, Norman. *The Doctrine of Deification in the Greek Patristic Tradition*. The Oxford Early Christian Studies. Oxford: Oxford University Press, 2006.

Schüle, Andreas. "Made in the 'Image of God': The Concepts of Divine Images in Gen 1–3." *Zeitschrift für die alttestamentliche Wissenschaft* 117 (2005) 1–20.

Sheppard, Phyllis Isabella. *Self, Culture, and Others in Womanist Practical Theology*. Black Religion/Womanist Thought/Social Justice. New York: Palgrave Macmillan, 2011.

Swann, John Thomas. *The Imago Dei: A Priestly Calling for Humankind*. Eugene, OR: Wipf & Stock, 2017.

Swinton, John. *Becoming Friends of Time: Disability, Timefulness, and Gentle Discipleship*. Studies in Religion, Theology, and Disability. London: SCM, 2016.

———. *Resurrecting the Person: Friendship and the Care of People with Mental Health Problems*. Nashville: Abingdon, 2000.

Tanner, Kathryn. *Christ the Key.* Current Issues in Theology. Cambridge: Cambridge University Press, 2010.

Thomas Aquinas. *Summa Theologica.* Translated by Fathers of the English Dominican Province. New York: Benzinger, 1948.

Thomas, Gabrielle. "The Human Icon: Gregory of Nazianzus on Being an Imago Dei." *Scottish Journal of Theology* 72 (2019) 166–81.

———. *The Image of God in the Theology of Gregory of Nazianzus.* Cambridge: Cambridge University Press, 2019.

———. "Vulnerable, Yet Divine: Retrieving Gregory Nazianzen's Account of the *Imago Dei*." In *The Christian Doctrine of Humanity: Explorations in Constructive Dogmatics,* edited by Oliver D. Crisp and Fred Sanders, 110–23. Grand Rapids: Zondervan, 2018.

Valerio, Ruth. *Just Living: Faith and Community in an Age of Consumerism.* London: Hodder & Stoughton, 2017.

———. *L is for Lifestyle: Christian Living That Doesn't Cost the Earth.* London: Inter-Varsity, 2019.

Vasari, Giorgio. *Lives of the Artists.* Translated by Julia Conway Bondanella and Peter Bondanella. Oxford World's Classics. Oxford: Oxford University Press, 2008.

Volf, Miraslov. *After Our Likeness: The Church as the Image of the Trinity.* Sacra Doctrina. Grand Rapids: Eerdmans. 1998.

Walton, John H. *The Lost World of Genesis One: Ancient Cosmology and the Origins Debate.* Downers Grove, IL: IVP Academic, 2009.

Yong, Amos. *The Bible, Disability, and the Church: A New Vision of the People of God.* Grand Rapids: Eerdmans, 2011.

Zizioulas, John D. *Being as Communion: Studies in Personhood and the Church.* Contemporary Greek Theologians 4. Crestwood, NY: St. Vladimir's Seminary Press, 1985.

AUTHOR INDEX

Author Index

Printed in Great Britain
by Amazon